To Write in the Light of Freedom

TO WRITE IN THE LIGHT OF FREEDOM

The Newspapers of the 1964 Mississippi Freedom Schools

Edited by

William Sturkey and Jon N. Hale

University Press of Mississippi / Jackson

Margaret Walker Alexander Series
in African American Studies

www.upress.state.ms.us

The University Press of Mississippi is a member
of the Association of American University Presses.

First printing 2015
∞
Library of Congress Cataloging-in-Publication Data

To write in the light of freedom : the newspapers of the 1964 Mississippi Freedom Schools / edited by William Sturkey and Jon N. Hale.
    pages cm — (Margaret Walker Alexander series in African American
studies)
    Includes index.
    "This collection contains Freedom School newspapers gathered from
archives, libraries, and personal collections across America"—Introduction.
    ISBN 978-1-62846-188-6 (hardback) — ISBN 978-1-62846-189-3 (ebook)
1. African Americans—Mississippi—Social conditions—20th century. 2.
African Americans—Civil rights—Mississippi—History—20th century. 3.
Civil rights movements—Mississippi—History—20th century. 4. Mississippi
Freedom Schools. 5. African American students—Mississippi—History—20th
century. 6. Student newspapers and periodicals—Mississippi—History—20th
century. I. Sturkey, William, editor of compilation. II. Hale, Jon N.
    E185.93.M6T6 2015
323.1196'07307620904—dc23   2014024113

British Library Cataloging-in-Publication Data available

*This book is dedicated to the courageous
individuals who attended and taught in the
Mississippi Freedom Schools during the summer of 1964.
Your vision and passion continues to inspire thousands.*

Contents

To Write in the Light of Freedom

Introduction

The Mississippi Freedom Schools changed lives. They opened doors for students, creating exciting new possibilities for thousands of young black Mississippians who attended them during the summer of 1964. Those eager young pupils, longing for equality and freedom, lived in a society still dominated by the unjust Jim Crow racial order that affected everything in their environment from schools to Coca-Cola machines to graveyards. That unbending system followed black Mississippians like shadows, constantly reminding that society had deemed them inferior. Daily events such as going to the movies, buying ice cream, or playing a ball game were haunted by "Whites Only" signs, heartless racial epithets, and the ever-present threat of violence. Jim Crow hovered over their lives and dreams, telling them "no" at every turn: no, they could not swim in the public pool; no, they could not take the school bus; no, they could not use the public library; and no, they would never be equal to the white children who lived across town. Freedom Schools offered something different. The Freedom Schools told them yes.

The Mississippi Freedom Schools were a series of voluntary schools conducted across the state during the summer of 1964. Organized by civil rights activists, Freedom Schools were designed to empower black Mississippi youths by supplementing their substandard public school educational opportunities with rigorous content and culturally relevant instruction. Still racially segregated a decade after the United States Supreme Court's 1954 *Brown v. Board of Education* decision, Mississippi's black and white public schools were extremely unequal. On average, the state spent about four times as much on white students as black pupils. Everything in the African American schools was inferior—desks, chairs, windows, bathrooms, chalkboards, even the books. Many black students only received hand-me-down

3

books from white schools. Every autumn, entire classes of black students opened the front cover of their textbooks only to find long lists of white students who had used the books when they were newer. As one African American student lamented, "This past term some of my books were as old as I." One of the most disturbing tales of educational inequality came from Ruleville. Every November in Ruleville, black students were loaded onto busses and forced to pick cotton for days on end. "I was 7 in the 3rd grade when I first went to the fields to pick," reported one African American student. The entire state was filled with heartbreaking tales of educational disparities. Thousands of black students simply did not have a chance. In November of 1963, civil rights organizer Charlie Cobb proposed "Freedom Schools" to help remedy the tragic educational disparities and develop a new generation of activists. He wanted to create spaces of equality and opportunity, or "Houses of Liberty," as one student later dubbed her Freedom School.[1]

Throughout the summer of 1964, black Mississippi youths rushed to the Freedom Schools in unexpected numbers, packing the churches and homes where the schools were being held. They came in droves because of the powerful educational and intellectual promise of Freedom School. Freedom Schools bolstered their students' self-esteem and expectations by connecting their lives to the rich traditions of black resistance and teaching them about the rights they were supposed to have as American citizens. The experience helped many young people develop a new way of thinking and a renewed confidence in their future. As fifteen-year-old Freedom School student Albert Evans explained, "Today I am the world's footstool but tomorrow I hope to be one of its leaders. By attending Freedom School this summer I am preparing for that tomorrow."[2] Throughout that summer, thousands of young African Americans like Albert arrived at the Freedom Schools ready to escape the boundaries of blackness in the Jim Crow South. By mid-July, over fifteen hundred students were enrolled in the Mississippi Freedom Schools. In the coming weeks they were joined by more than a thousand of their peers. Most of their lives would never be the same.

The experiences and voices of those hopeful Mississippi Freedom School students are captured in the following pages. Their own words are published here as part of an unprecedented collection of articles, essays, poems, and testimonies written by Freedom School students during the summer of 1964. After a brief introduction that offers a broader context and defines key historical moments in the Civil Rights Movement, this book contains hundreds of writings published in a series of newspapers produced by Freedom School students. By publishing their works, this primary source collection highlights those students' voices and displays their powerful responses to life in the Jim Crow South, the Civil Rights Movement, and the legendary Freedom Schools themselves, offering today's readers a unique view into the transformative power of Freedom Schools through the eyes of the inspirational students who spent their summers in those "Houses of Liberty," learning, growing, and dreaming as they never had before.[3]

The Background of Jim Crow and Education in Mississippi

In the summer of 1964, a coalition of Mississippi-based civil rights organizations launched perhaps the most ambitious campaign of the entire Civil Rights Movement. Together, they set out to "crack" Mississippi, the nation's most racially oppressive state. Black Mississippians had been fighting for greater freedoms since Emancipation. For nearly a century, they had been building, developing, and organizing strong communities to improve their lives under the brutal specter of Jim Crow. Optimism increased during World War II when America seemingly took a firm stance against racism. Thousands of black Mississippians joined the fight for international democracy and returned from serving their country overseas expecting to enjoy the promises of democracy at home. But they were met by white supremacists who fiercely defended Jim Crow. Still, black communities continued fighting for social equality, the right to vote, and better educational opportunities for their children. In 1960, these courageous local activists received a major boost when a representative from a civil rights organization named the Student Nonviolent Coordinating Committee (SNCC) arrived in Mississippi looking for ways to help. Four years later, that swelling coalition of local and external civil rights activists brought thousands of reinforcements from across America into Mississippi as part of an epic civil rights campaign known as Freedom Summer. It was an exciting new phase in a long struggle.

Mississippi's modern white supremacist order began taking shape in 1875 when self-armed groups of white vigilantes organized to expel African Americans from the voting rolls. During the Reconstruction era that followed the Civil War, black Mississippians had been granted full citizenship, the right to vote (for males), and access to public school education. These newfound rights infuriated thousands of white Mississippians who had only known the old racial order created by slavery. The Civil War set those former slaves free, and some of the former bondspeople were even thriving, rising higher in society than many poor whites. Two African Americans—Hiram Revels and Bruce Blanche—had even become United States senators. On top of that, virtually all newly enfranchised black citizens voted Republican, further drawing the ire of many white southerners who despised the "Party of Lincoln." Resolving to reestablish Democratic political rule and racial domination, the state's most ardent white supremacists began organizing small vigilante groups that met in secret to plan for change. As historian Vernon Lane Wharton has written, these organizations had one goal: "the restoration of white supremacy in Mississippi." Their efforts culminated on election day in 1875.[4]

On November 2, 1875, the vigilante groups and their allies—collectively known as the "Redeemers"—successfully regained control over the state legislature. They used any means necessary to ensure a sweeping political victory, arriving at polling places with guns or cannons to intimidate Republican voters, stuffing ballot boxes, and attacking would-be black voters. Some African Americans who tried to cast ballots were even killed. The federal government, weary from nearly fifteen years of war and occupation, sat idly by as Mississippi's Redeemers overthrew the state's Republican Party.[5]

The success of the Mississippi Revolution of 1875 inspired similar white supremacist uprisings across the South. The following year saw massive electoral fraud and violence against black voters in states such as Florida, Louisiana, and South Carolina, leading to a compromise that ultimately ended Reconstruction. In 1877, President Rutherford B. Hayes withdrew federal troops from the South, leaving millions of African Americans, just over a decade out of slavery, to fend for themselves. A new standardized form of white supremacy crept over the region. White legislators passed strict segregation laws and repealed many of the political gains made by African Americans after Emancipation. The coming years saw the rise of Jim Crow, a brutal racial order that separated black and white southerners in nearly all aspects of society and excluded African Americans from the finest opportunities of the oncoming twentieth century.[6]

Mississippi's black public school system was hit particularly hard by the emergence of Jim Crow. Five years before the Revolution of 1875, black Mississippi legislators and their Republican allies had created the South's first public school system for African Americans. Black Mississippians had always desired education. Even during the antebellum era, thousands of enslaved African Americans broke the law by learning to read and write. Worried about enslaved people's ability to forge passes or communicate between plantations, white slave owners forbade their field hands to gain literacy. But the bondspeople strove to learn anyway. They smuggled newspapers and books into slave quarters and taught each other to read whenever they got the chance. One young former slave named Isaiah Montgomery remembered spending nights reading a contraband copy of *Uncle Tom's Cabin* to his fellow bondsmen who greatly appreciated the boy's willingness to share his literacy.[7]

Immediately after the Civil War, African Americans flocked to schools run by the Freedmen's Bureau, a government organization in charge of overseeing the transition of bondspeople from slavery to freedom. These Freedmen's Bureau schools were enormously popular across Mississippi. Entire black communities turned out to attend and support them. Others actually established their own independent school systems when the Freedmen's Bureau schools did not fully meet their needs. Literacy was a practical matter for the freedpeople. It allowed them to sign land deeds, analyze work contracts, and read the Bible. Learning also made them citizens, enabling them to follow political developments and cast ballots. For many, reading was a status symbol. Among an entire generation of former slaves who had been systematically kept illiterate, those who could read were often held in high esteem.[8]

In 1870, black Mississippi legislators established a permanent public school system for African Americans to replace the temporary Freedmen's Bureau schools. These new public schools were not racially integrated. They were, however, designed to be equal. The initial Mississippi public school mandate called for "separate free public schools for whites and colored pupils" with "the same and equal advantages and immunities under the provision of this act." Black legislators included a series of protective clauses to ensure that African American students enjoyed similar educational opportunities as their white counterparts. The act included a provision that read, "whenever any county, municipal, corporation, or school district shall fail to provide separate schools for white and colored pupils, with the same and equal advantages," the responsible parties "shall be punished by a fine of not less than two hundred dollars, nor more than five hundred dollars, and by imprisonment in the county jail, for not less than three months." Additionally, the act stated that "such persons so offending shall also be liable to an action for damages by the parent or guardian of the pupil so refused." These penalties made racially unequal school funding a fairly serious crime, one publishable by a large fine, imprisonment, and even civil lawsuits. But like any law, the new public school regulations were only effective if enforced. After Mississippi's white Redeemers claimed power in 1875, no legislator dared to even suggest that the state enforce racial equality in public schools. In fact, they did just the opposite.[9]

Almost immediately after the Revolution of 1875, Mississippi's new Democratic-controlled state legislature began diverting resources from black public schools. The first action they took was to change the leadership. In February of 1876, Mississippi

Superintendent of Education Thomas Cardoza, an African American, was accused of embezzling over $18,000 in school funds (the historical equivalent of approximately $360,000) and forced to resign before being impeached or murdered.[10] He was replaced by a white Democrat named T. S. Gathright, who once called Mississippi's black public school system "an unmitigated outrage upon the rights and liberties of the white people of the State."[11] Gathright began making drastic cuts, especially to black teachers' salaries. In just one year, the average monthly salaries of black teachers dropped from $53.45 to $38.54. By 1890, teachers in black schools were paid only $23.20 per month, less than half of what they had earned twenty years before. All aspects of school funding experienced similar reductions. Every year, white Mississippi legislators gave less and less to support the state's black public schools. Other discriminatory measures followed.[12]

In 1889, African American teachers were expelled from the Mississippi Educational Association, the state's professional teaching organization.[13] Legislators also enacted strict control over school lessons. They removed large sections of African American history from schoolbooks. New textbooks commonly ignored the history of Reconstruction-era black leaders and often depicted slavery as an essential, sometimes even pleasant, social device designed to ease the transition of Africans into a Christian democracy. Black teachers who discussed radical African American heroes or cast slavery in a negative light were quickly dismissed and barred from teaching in the Mississippi public schools. During a process that historians have often dubbed "counter Reconstruction," white Mississippi legislators stripped African American schools of their resources and established strict control over their curricula, limiting the once-promising educational opportunities of black public schools.[14]

Black Mississippians struggled to preserve the promise of education. In what historian James Anderson has labeled "double taxation," many African American communities used their own resources to subsidize the underfunded black schools. They repaired and maintained schoolhouses, joined Parent-Teacher Associations, and donated time and money. But they could only do so much. Despite their efforts, the stark realities of racially discriminatory spending just simply crippled many black schools. The effects lingered across generations. As historian Christopher Span has concluded, "The schools that African American children would attend from 1880 until the late 1960s would primarily educate them for a life of second-class citizenship and servitude."[15]

In 1890, Mississippi's predominantly white legislative body convened to formally remove African American political rights. Although the Mississippi Revolution of 1875 was effective in disfranchising most black voters, the tactics of violence and intimidation were also illegal. Technically, African Americans were still legally guaranteed the right to vote by the 15th Amendment, which the state had ratified in 1870 as a precondition for rejoining the Union. Therefore, denying black citizens the right to vote was illegal, even if the federal government turned a blind eye to disfranchisement. To *legally* remove African Americans from voter rolls, Mississippi legislators gathered in 1890 to produce a new state constitution.[16]

Mississippi's new constitution included a redefined public school law that mandated racially segregated schools, but left out any discussion of equality. It also outlined several new voting laws, including one that required citizens to pay a poll tax in order to register. Of particular significance to black Mississippians was Article XII, Section 244 of the new Mississippi Constitution. It stated that all voters "be able to read any section of the constitution of this State" and "be able to understand the same when read to him, or give a reasonable interpretation thereof." This "understanding clause" was written into the Mississippi Constitution of 1890 specifically to control African American political activity. Without any sort of standardized measurement of one's ability to "understand" or "interpret" the new constitution, individual registrars were given the power to decide who could qualify to vote. And by 1890, nearly every single registrar in the state of Mississippi was a white Democrat. This new measure did not remove all African Americans from the voter rolls, but it did lay the groundwork for individual registrars to deny any black person the right to vote if that person did not properly interpret a section of the state constitution or if for whatever reason the white registrar simply did not want a particular individual to vote. The disfranchisement methods were extremely effective, and over the course of seventy years, millions of black Mississippians were excluded from the promises of American democracy.[17]

◆　◆　◆

Sixty years after the Constitutional Convention of 1890, Mississippi's black public schools remained tragically neglected. Because white Democrats prohibited African Americans from voting and thus electing sympathetic legislators and school administrators, black Mississippians had virtually no influence over the state's educational resources. Most white Mississippi legislators cared little about African American education and set aside very few resources for black public schools. As historian Leon Litwack has observed, "[N]o state gave less to black education between 1890 and World War II."[18]

Through the 1940s and 1950s, black Mississippi schools were among the worst public institutions in America. They were often run-down, overcrowded, and always inferior, even to the state's poor white schools which had problems of their own. Black Mississippi students had older books, substandard facilities, fewer supplies, and smaller playgrounds than their white counterparts. Some districts did not even offer classes beyond the eighth grade, forcing African Americans to either drop out or move away from their families to complete high school. Other districts conformed their school calendars to the cotton harvest schedule, ensuring the availability of African American youths to work in cotton fields of rich, white planters. (This arrangement also helped some impoverished black families that desperately needed income.) Even after World War II, when the rest of America stood on the cusp of its most prosperous era, many black Mississippi students attended schools in unheated, crumbling wooden shacks. Among the poorest populations in America, black Mississippi students also had the fewest opportunities because they had been born in a state that gave them so little.[19]

But of course Mississippi did not exist in a vacuum. Through much of the twentieth century, powerful forces of change were gathering across America. In the 1930s and 1940s, the National Association for the Advancement of Colored People (NAACP) began a full-scale legal campaign against racially based educational inequalities in American public schools. These early efforts included battles to equalize teacher salaries, gain access to state-funded law schools, and equal treatment for African Americans attending public institutions of higher learning. Gladys Noel Bates, a black science teacher in Jackson, sued the local school district to equalize her salary.[20] White school officials terminated her teaching contract, which sent a powerful message to those who wished to challenge Jim Crow. But activists were undeterred. In a series of Supreme Court decisions, the NAACP and its talented team of lawyers began peeling back the legality of racially segregated schools by proving that segregation was inherently unequal, a fact black Mississippians knew all too well. Culminating with the famous 1954 *Brown v. Board of Education* ruling, these Supreme Court cases directly threatened the South's racially segregated public school systems.[21]

Because the United States Supreme Court ordered that school desegregation be conducted at "all deliberate speed," many white Mississippi officials believed they could avoid integration by allocating more resources to black schools. In a last-ditch effort to prove that the old adage of "separate but equal" could work, legislators earmarked millions of dollars to build and improve black schools. Yet, even these efforts were limited by racial discrimination. Some city and county officials, succumbing to long-standing prejudices and local political pressure, simply refused to distribute funds equally. Therefore, despite some cosmetic improvements, the quality of African American schools never approached that of the white ones. As late as 1962, many Mississippi counties were still spending far more money on white students. For example, the Amite County district spent an average of $70.45 and $2.24 on white and black students, respectively. In Tunica County the average per-pupil school expenditure was $172.80 for white pupils and a mere $5.99 for African Americans. Mississippi's black and white schools never approached equalization. African American students remained severely disadvantaged.[22]

Meanwhile, as white politicians scrambled to avoid school integration, a growing mass of black Mississippi leaders were organizing for change. These men and women, coming together in the face of intense physical, economic, and emotional threats, were focused primarily on securing the right to vote. They knew that the power of the ballot could fundamentally alter their lives. Beyond the sheer appeal of participating in the American democracy, gaining the vote could allow black communities to elect officials who would help provide more resources for their neighborhoods, better access to health care, and, of course, better schools for their children. By the mid-1950s, hundreds of these like-minded individuals were organized into a grassroots localized network led by Medgar Wiley Evers, Mississippi's first NAACP field secretary. After fighting in World War II, Evers spent nearly a decade of his life organizing small groups of brave black Mississippians who resolved to fight for voting rights despite the potentially severe consequences of challenging Jim Crow. Their gains were small but encouraging.[23]

In the early 1960s, Mississippi's courageous black freedom fighters received an injection of energy when waves of young activists from the Student Nonviolent Coordinating Committee (SNCC) arrived in the state to help organize local people to pursue the right to vote. This coalition of freedom fighters fanned out across the state, holding mass meetings and demonstrations in black communities where they encouraged everyday African Americans to try and register to vote. There were successes and inspiring moments, but activists were also met with an intense resistance from white segregationists.[24]

White supremacists organized at all levels—from the governor to the Ku Klux Klan—to resist any form of racial integration or equality. Local black activists and SNCC workers were arrested, beaten, and sometimes even killed. Civil rights organizers constantly appealed to the federal government for help, but the Kennedy administration, distracted by the Cold War and concerned about maintaining the allegiance of southern Democrats, offered only empty calculated gestures that did little to protect black Mississippians who were fighting for their basic constitutional rights. Activists working in Mississippi knew they had to do something drastic to attract more national attention and federal protection that would help lift the veil of fear preventing most black Mississippians from joining the movement. As SNCC staff member Charles Cobb recalled, "You had to bring the country's attention to the state, and the obvious way to do that is to bring the country's children down there. You make Mississippi a big campaign— you nationalize Mississippi, essentially, by bringing America's children to Mississippi. Nobody can ignore the state then."[25]

During the winter and spring of 1963 and 1964, SNCC workers spread across the country to recruit "America's children" to Mississippi for an ambitious campaign they initially called the "Summer Project." Grizzled from years of struggling against America's most severe form of white supremacy, veteran activists arrived on campuses of universities such as Yale, Stanford, and Princeton to recruit mostly white college students to spend a summer fighting for black rights in Mississippi. Many of the students were liberal, ambitious, and gifted. Most were also privileged. They had come of age during the most prosperous era in American history and enjoyed advantages unimaginable to most black Mississippians. But these young people were also idealistic and conscientious. Over the preceding years, they had seen the Civil Rights Movement expose ugly truths about the limitations of America for southern African Americans. Virtually all of the white students had seen dozens of disturbing images from the South. On newsstands and television sets, they saw scenes from Oxford, Mississippi, in 1962 when the enrollment of African American student James Meredith incited a riot at the University of Mississippi. In 1963, they had seen terrifying images of fire hoses spraying young children in the streets of Birmingham, Alabama. And just weeks later, they had also seen the devastatingly sad *LIFE* magazine cover photograph of Medgar Evers's widow, Myrlie, comforting her teary-eyed son at her assassinated husband's funeral. With the South wrapped in racial chaos, many of those bright-eyed college students genuinely wanted to help make America a better place.[26]

Most veteran Mississippi activists held reservations about bringing "sympathetic" outsiders to help organize local African Americans, especially if those outsiders were white. Many stressed that black Mississippians needed to lead the protests if the movement were to have a long-term impact. After all, it was Mississippi's local black residents who would remain in the state and carry on the freedom struggle long after the outsiders left. But by the spring of 1964, most of those concerns were cast aside in lieu of the importance of drawing federal protection for civil rights workers in Mississippi. In January of 1964, yet another black freedom fighter named Louis Allen had been murdered, and activists knew that the federal government would go to greater lengths to protect privileged white college students than it had ever done to help black Mississippians. The students were going to come, and they were indeed going to bring much of America's attention with them. Mississippi's numerous civil rights groups organized under an umbrella organization called the Council of Federated Organizations (COFO) to conduct the campaign.[27]

As they planned Freedom Summer, several veteran civil rights activists began thinking of ways to expand and supplement voter registration efforts. From years of living, working, and struggling in Mississippi, SNCC workers had been exposed to the severe limitations of the state's black public school system. Many were stunned at the lack of education among black Mississippians. When SNCC first arrived in Mississippi, only 4.2 percent of the state's African American population over the age of twenty-five held high school diplomas.[28] Many adults did not know how to read. Others did not know basic facts such as how many states composed the United States of America. Even ten years after *Brown v. Board of Education*, some black Mississippians had never even heard of the famous Supreme Court decision that had supposedly integrated America's schools. The educational disadvantages afflicting most black Mississippians were both heartbreaking and obvious. Although SNCC was primarily focused on voter registration, politics and education were clearly connected, just as they had always been in Mississippi. Those educational inequalities were a direct result of the systematic racial disfranchisement that had taken place nearly a century prior.[29]

In November of 1963, Charles Cobb sent a memo describing the vast educational and intellectual poverty infecting thousands of black Mississippians. To offer a remedy for some, Cobb proposed a system of "Freedom Schools" to be conducted across the state during the upcoming Summer Project. Rooted in well-established organizing traditions, the schools would provide an opportunity to use white student volunteers' prestigious educational pedigrees to teach young black Mississippians. Several organizers also envisioned Freedom Schools as a way to stymie the historical stream of African Americans who left Mississippi for better opportunities elsewhere. In order to combat a "brain drain" effect in local communities, Freedom Summer activists planned to focus on "tenth- and eleventh-grade high school students," many of whom were considering whether to stay or leave the Magnolia State for good. Cobb also saw these independent schools as pathways for young people into the movement. Freedom Schools, he argued, could "supplement what they aren't learning in high schools," "give them a broad intellectual and academic experience," and "form the basis for statewide student action." And thus the Freedom School idea was born.[30]

The ambitious Freedom School idea must be considered within the broader context of the historic freedom struggle of black Mississippians, especially considering the long-term connection between politics and education. Since the Revolution of 1875, Mississippi's white supremacist leaders had robbed black students of educational resources and opportunities. The Freedom Schools of 1964 represented not just an innovative new movement strategy, but also symbolized the recovery of a lost promise made to a people nearly one hundred years before. Whether the activists, students, or teachers knew it or not, they were reviving a dream that had been deferred for nearly a century. Those who volunteered to teach in the Mississippi Freedom Schools during the 1964 Freedom Summer were joining an explosive social movement, but the young black students who arrived for those classes were part of a much deeper struggle.

Education and the Civil Rights Movement

Education and social activism were always connected. The Freedom School idea itself was particularly rooted in longstanding traditions of American liberalism, especially through the political, economic, and social education model pioneered by Highlander Folk School founder Myles Horton during the Great Depression. Horton, a progressive white liberal from eastern Tennessee, founded Highlander in the foothills of the Tennessee Smokey Mountains after spending years studying with Progressive-era educational reformers such as John Dewey, Jane Addams, George Counts, and Reinhold Niebuhr. Deeply committed to social justice and civic equality, Horton based his school's educational philosophy on participatory democracy ideologies. Students were to participate in developing their own educational experience and play active roles in shaping classroom curriculums to meet their varying political and economic needs. In essence, Highlander's flexible pedagogy helped allow marginalized people to facilitate their own paths to liberation.[31]

Throughout the 1930s and 1940s, Highlander Folk School served as a crucial training ground for labor and social justice activists. In the postwar era, Highlander became more involved with America's increasingly explosive racial issue. African American activists, many of whom had direct connections with labor organizers, were mobilizing across the country to protest various forms of discrimination. The alliance of race and labor drew Horton's school into a burgeoning movement. Highlander's first, and perhaps most important, contribution to the Civil Rights Movement was the development of Citizenship Schools.[32]

The idea for Citizenship Schools originated during a 1955 Highlander workshop on the United Nations. Among this workshop's attendees were Esau Jenkins and Septima Poinsette Clark. Jenkins was a small landowner from John's Island, South Carolina, who regularly supplemented his income by transporting working-class black islanders to and from the mainland. Through years of living among and working with illiterate and impoverished black workers who held no political power, Jenkins became acutely aware of the problems facing his neighbors and began thinking of ways to help them improve their lives. During these trips, he began discussing, reading, and writing passages drawn from the state constitution with some of his passengers, effectively gauging their knowledge and eventually providing some with basic literacy tools. But Jenkins wanted to do even more to help. He wanted to reach the masses of poor people he saw struggling in the South, and so he arrived at Highlander to share his challenges and gain ideas. Septima Clark, an educator from Charleston who had previously taught on John's Island, was already active in the Civil Rights Movement. As a member of the South Carolina NAACP, she was actively involved in the organization's fight to equalize teacher salaries in black and white schools. Clark lost her teaching job because of her commitment to the movement, but found a like-minded ally in Esau Jenkins. When the pair went to Tennessee, the story of their experiences quickly drew the interest of Myles Horton and others at the Highlander Folk School.[33]

Jenkins returned home with a plan to open an education center where locals could learn to read, write, and register to vote. Clark returned to John's Island to help establish a location, find a teacher, and recruit students. The first school was established in the back of a recently purchased grocery store. It was taught by Clark's niece, Bernice Robinson, a local black beautician who opened the first day of class with just fourteen students, some pencils and paper, and a copy of the United Nation's Declaration of Human Rights.[34] Those humble beginnings were the start of something much bigger to come. The power of education for liberation drew widespread interest, and word of the first Citizenship School at John's Island gradually spread through other southern black communities. People interested in starting their own Citizenship Schools were invited to the Highlander Folk School for training. These new teachers then trained others.

Rooted in the Highlander model, Citizenship Schools were explicitly political. The literacy skills taught in Citizenship Schools were specifically designed to enable older African Americans to pass voter registration requirements. A common "test" at the end of a two-to-three-month Citizenship School session was for students to attempt to register to vote at the local precinct. During the late 1950s and early 1960s, the schools spread through Dixie, training thousands of southern African Americans and drawing them into the Civil Rights Movement. By 1965, more than fifty thousand registered voters had been trained in nearly nine hundred Citizenship Schools across the South.[35]

Citizenship Schools built on previously existing traditions in southern black communities. They were merely the most recent manifestation of education for liberation, an important connection that had existed since the antebellum era when enslaved African Americans learned to read in secret, dreaming of ways education could one day help them improve their lives, find lost family members, and gain freedom. The former black slaves continued their educational quest during the Reconstruction era, flocking to Freedmen's Bureau schools and even starting many of their own. Those who managed to graduate high school and even college often returned to their communities to help lead and teach. Black educators and professionals emerged as the "talented tenth" during the era of Jim Crow. This cadre of talented African Americans provided the leadership and vision that helped lay the educational foundations of the Civil Rights Movement.

During the Jim Crow era, women committed to education such as Septima Clark, Ella Baker, Gladys Noel Bates, and countless others helped cultivate the seeds of the Civil Rights Movement by guiding communities and young people to mobilize for collective action within neighborhood schools. Though often working behind the scenes, thousands of African American educators in the Jim Crow South helped generate widespread communal support for local schools, fought to equalize teacher salaries, and tried to increase the amount of resources allocated to black schools. Many also later became involved with the Citizenship Schools that spread across the South during the late 1950s. Educational activism built upon decades of an organic struggle for knowledge among black families who had long associated education with political freedom and liberation. Learning at all levels, including high school and college in both the public and private sectors, provided the foundation of political socialization in southern black schools.[36]

As the Civil Rights Movement spread across Dixie, long-standing educational traditions in southern black communities combined with a growing political renaissance to generate early versions of Freedom Schools—alternative educational institutions that promoted racial equality. In 1961, fifteen-year-old African American student Brenda Travis was expelled from McComb's Burgland High School for participating in civil rights activities. Her peers walked out and formed an alternative school they dubbed "Nonviolent High" to protest Travis's expulsion. In 1963, organizers in Virginia's Prince Edward County formed their own versions of "Freedom Schools" in response to the local school district closing public schools to avoid racial integration. Several other versions of Freedom Schools opened in the North. During the winter of 1964, Boston educators led by Noel Day conducted a school boycott to protest de facto segregation in the city's public schools. On February 26, 1964, hundreds of student protestors attended the Boston "Freedom Schools" and received Freedom Diplomas for their participation. New York City activists similarly organized their own versions of Freedom Schools during the spring of 1964. As COFO activists began planning the 1964 Mississippi Freedom Schools, they found several examples of other Freedom School–type programs to build upon. The biggest difference was scale. The 1964 Mississippi Freedom Schools were going to involve a lot more students than any other similar program. But the basic dogma of education for liberation and citizenship was already well established, both within local black communities and among veterans of the movement.[37]

Freedom School Curriculum

In March of 1964, a talented collection of educators and civil rights activists gathered in New York City to plan the Freedom School curriculum. This assembly was sponsored by the National Council of Churches, which had made a serious commitment the previous spring to begin supporting the Civil Rights Movement. Conference attendees included veteran activists such as Bayard Rustin and Andrew Young, Citizenship School pioneers Septima Clark and Myles Horton, several experienced New York City public school teachers, and a number of seasoned educational activists, including Noel Day. The primary objective of the New York conference was to create a full curriculum for Freedom

Summer volunteers to follow in their classrooms. Writing a curriculum to use in the Freedom Schools was critically important. Curriculum planners knew that many of the volunteer Freedom School teachers had never taught before and needed a bulk of material to help them prepare for classes.[38]

Conference attendees met in a large body before breaking into smaller groups based on personal specializations to design the various aspects of the Freedom School curriculum. The groups met for two days to discuss and plan the ambitious curriculum. Attendees left those small meetings charged with producing teaching materials that could be used as parts of the official curriculum. Instructional approaches and lesson plans were to be mailed back to Freedom School organizers and then integrated into a single, comprehensive curriculum. Many of the curriculum writers contributed various lesson plans and strategies that were used to form an official Freedom School curriculum guide.[39]

As the curriculum guide stated, the Freedom Schools served to "sharpen the students' abilities to read, write, work mathematical problems, etc. but [also to] concentrate more on stimulating a student's interest in learning, finding his [sic] special abilities, so that when he returns to the state schools in the fall he can take maximum advantage of the public education which is offered to him."[40] Toward this end, the Curriculum Conference Report adopted behavioral outcomes that were grounded in traditional learning objectives. For instance, the students were expected "to develop his [sic] sense of self-worth and self-confidence in his ability to learn, achieve and contribute . . . to improve his ability to communicate ideas . . . to improve his study habits and skills . . . to promote his sensitivity to and competence in the use of logical thinking, critical judgment and problem-solving processes . . . to develop his skills and competence in handling money and financial transaction."[41]

The official Freedom School curriculum was composed of three parts. Part II, the "Citizenship Curriculum," was by far the largest and most important portion of the Freedom School curriculum. It opened by reiterating that "[o]ne of the purposes of the Freedom Schools is to train people to be active agents in bringing about social change." The Citizenship Curriculum was divided into seven units. The first section offered a series of prompts that asked students to begin comparing their realities with those of others, especially local whites, and begin discussing ways to improve their own lives. The second portion of the Citizenship Curriculum introduced them to the Mississippi power structure by explaining how their society worked and the ways the movement had been trying to combat the systematic racism of Jim Crow. This section was crucial. Freedom School planners understood that although young black students knew that racial inferiority was unjust, they did not necessarily understand why or how those inequalities had been constructed. By understanding basic processes, such as how local officials were elected or appointed, they would be able to develop an understanding of how to change aspects of their society. Other units of the Citizenship Curriculum included lessons on Mississippi politics, the Mississippi Freedom Democratic Party (MFDP), and the recent history of civil rights activism in the state. Overall, the broad goal of the Citizenship Curriculum was to teach the young Freedom School students about the institutionalized racism of their society and develop in them a basic civic literacy so they could understand how various movement tactics challenged existing structures.[42]

Although standard academic components were less visible in the Freedom School curriculum than overt political objectives, they were just as important. Part I of the Freedom School curriculum emphasized standard academic instruction, especially reading, writing, and mathematical skills, and included activities such as oral reading, writing discussion summaries, composing poetry, reading newspapers, and some basic arithmetic exercises. The third and final part of the Freedom School curriculum was a smaller section titled "Recreational and Artistic" that emphasized fostering artistic skills and active play.[43] Freedom Schools were designed to balance political objectives with standard educational goals. Students were instructed in basic lessons on American government, history, and reading and writing skills. The curriculum also included an emphasis on African American literature, history, and culture, topics that had been censured for decades in many of the state's regular black public schools.

The study of African American history was particularly important. Freedom School coordinator Staughton Lynd, a Columbia University–trained historian, prepared a unit called the "Guide to Negro History," which included brief lessons on the history of slavery, Reconstruction, and Jim Crow. It also incorporated sections on historical black leaders such as Gabriel Prosser, Nat Turner, and Frederick Douglass. With regular Mississippi public schools censoring discussions of aggressive African American leaders, Lynd thought that Freedom Schools could help young black students develop a sense of pride in the accomplishments and history of their race through an exposure to deep-rooted radical traditions in the black freedom struggle. Staughton Lynd wrote brief synopses of major events in African American history and encouraged Freedom School teachers to share the historical information with their students. Those history lessons proved valuable to the development of Freedom School students. As is evidenced throughout their newspaper articles, essays, and poems, students embraced African American historical figures and used the lessons from the past to reinforce their hopes for the future.[44]

Although the curriculum guide was important as a pedagogical baseline, it was never intended to completely dictate the parameters of classroom instruction and learning. Rather, it was designed to be used as a resource for teachers who needed support. As Freedom School coordinator Staughton Lynd explained, the guide itself "was like a security blanket. When you ran out of things to do with the kids, you might get out the old Freedom School curriculum and think 'Oh, I can do that tomorrow.'" As Lynd later elaborated, "[I]t was therefore a backup. But most of what happened in the schools was improvised."[45] The content and style of teaching closely mirrored the earlier educational models of participatory education espoused at the Highlander Folk School and the Citizenship School program.

The curriculum guide was important to many teachers, especially those without any formal instructional experience or training. Alongside the various parts and units, it offered examples of a potential classroom schedule, lists of questions to generate student discussion, and also basic information on topics such as

African American history and the history of the movement in Mississippi. Many of the teachers themselves did not have strong backgrounds in African American history and were challenged by the new material. In these cases the curriculum became an important instructional guide. "A lot of what I was teaching, I never knew about," explained Freedom School teacher Stanley Zibulsky, "because we didn't get really to study black history [in public schools] . . . It took a lot of studying to just be able to teach." Despite not always having strong backgrounds in each topic, Freedom School teachers learned what they could and passed the lessons on to their students.[46]

The Freedom School curriculum guide was also an important way of stressing the pedagogical approach to political education pioneered by Myles Horton at the Highlander Folk School. Horton was one of the attendees at the New York City Curriculum Conference and his influence on the curriculum was clear. Freedom School classes were going to resemble participatory democracies aimed at developing strategies for social change. Teachers were to facilitate dialogue while students guided the learning process and produced answers. The curriculum guide included a "Basic Set of Questions" that asked Freedom School students to consider why they were in Freedom School and how the Civil Rights Movement might change their lives. Other questions asked students to compare white and black schools, housing, employment, and medical facilities, constantly asking students to define the parameters of their oppression and consider measures that would make their society more equal.[47]

A major part of the Freedom School mission was to fold young black students into the black freedom movement and encourage a cadre of young local leaders who could help lead civil rights activism well after the end of Freedom Summer. As the original proposal stated, Freedom Schools were conceived to train students who could "form the basis for statewide student action such as school boycotts, based on their increased awareness." Just as Myles Horton had once done with Highlander and Septima Clark had implemented with Citizenship Schools, the 1964 Mississippi Freedom Schools were designed to empower a new generation of people who could carry the fight forward.[48]

Freedom Summer and the Opening of Freedom Schools

For most Freedom School teachers, the Mississippi Freedom Summer actually began in Ohio. After applying, being accepted, and committing to the summer project, volunteers attended a week-long orientation on the campus of Western College for Women in Oxford, Ohio (now a part of Miami University). The week in Ohio was crucial for Freedom School teachers. They spent the week meeting new colleagues and learning basic movement skills such as ways to absorb an attack, how to respond to an arrest, and the words to dozens of freedom songs. Freedom School teachers studied the curriculum and listened to seasoned activists talk about how to interact with the black Mississippi youths who would be attending Freedom Schools. During that week, Freedom School organizers also completed a great deal of administrative work. They spent hours organizing school staffs, distributing curriculums, and making housing preparations. For many volunteers, the experience in Oxford also served as an important emotional transition between their prior lives and the intense racial climate they were about to enter. Mississippi's racial order was dangerous and terrifying, a fact confirmed to volunteers when Bob Moses took the stage during an orientation session and announced that three civil rights workers—James Chaney, a local African American Mississippian involved with Congress of Racial Equality (CORE), Mickey Schwerner, a white CORE staff member from New York, and Andrew Goodman, a white Freedom Summer volunteer who had been in Mississippi just one day—had disappeared and were presumed dead.[49] The three missing workers had been in Oxford just days before and their disappearance frightened both seasoned and new activists. Yet, most resolved to continue on to Mississippi and spent the rest of orientation preparing for the summer and coming to terms with internal conflicts between hope and fear. Meanwhile, as the mainly white northern volunteers prepared to enter the nation's most racially oppressive state, hundreds of young black Mississippi youths waited anxiously for the opening of the Freedom Schools.[50]

By the time Freedom School classes began in the first week of July, hundreds of students were already enrolled. In Hattiesburg alone, nearly six hundred African Americans preregistered for Freedom School classes. Similar, albeit smaller, reactions were common elsewhere. Plenty of young black Mississippians had previously participated in movement activities, but most had never enjoyed any form of leadership role. Too young to vote, their activism consisted primarily of filling the pulpits and following others. Many saw Freedom Schools as their pathway to full involvement or leadership and rushed to the schools in large numbers. Within just three weeks, Freedom School attendance figures more than doubled the expected enrollment for the entire summer. Students arrived at the schools bursting with energy, each ready to learn, grow, and join the fight for racial equality. Their fervor surprised many volunteers. As one Freedom School teacher reported, "The atmosphere in class is unbelievable. It is what every teacher dreams about—real, honest enthusiasm and desire to learn anything and everything." "The students couldn't get enough," remembered Palmer's Crossing–based teacher Sandra Adickes, "they wanted more; they wanted as much as I could give them."[51]

By late July, Freedom School organizers counted 41 official schools with a total attendance of 2,135 students. The typical school consisted of between 25 to 100 students taught by 5 or 6 teachers. Some schools, such as the Meridian Freedom School, were larger. Some cities, most notably Hattiesburg, had more than one Freedom School. The precise number of schools that operated that summer is hard to track. All summer long, improvised Freedom Schools opened across the state, even in places where no school had been planned. Freedom School administrators had only planned for 25 schools, but many communities heard of the program and decided to organize their own schools. Some lasted just a week or two. Others carried on into the autumn and through the next school year. COFO supplied teachers when possible, but there was always a shortage of instructors. The exact number of Freedom School students is similarly hard to accurately measure. Some students attended regularly, but others came only when they were free from work or able to escape their parents' watchful eye. Not all parents wanted their children to attend Freedom School due to potential repercussions from white supremacists.

During the previous years, thousands of black Mississippians had been fired from their jobs or attacked for participating in movement activities. All black families were very familiar with the risks associated with joining the movement. Because of this very real threat, not every Freedom School kept attendance or precise records of student enrollment. Those lists could be extremely dangerous if they fell into the wrong hands.[52]

The Freedom Schools received widespread support from within Mississippi and across the country. Local African Americans donated most of the land and structures used for Freedom School classes, a risky venture since all buildings known for supporting civil rights activities were under constant threat from white supremacists. Black Mississippi adults cleared areas for Freedom School classes, cleaned and painted classrooms, delivered daily lunches, transported students, housed teachers, and even at times protected the schools from attacks. Local African Americans also opened their homes to Freedom Summer volunteers, organizing places for them to stay and feeding them all summer long. Those interracial interactions in black homes and neighborhoods had a major impact on everyone involved and created lasting relationships between people from completely different backgrounds. Fifty years later, many of the African American hosts are still in contact with the volunteers they helped house during the 1964 Freedom Summer. Without the support of local black communities, the Mississippi Freedom Schools would not have been nearly as widespread, well organized, or productive.[53]

Freedom Schools were also bolstered by a great deal of outside support, especially in the form of material donations. COFO needed all sorts of provisions to run what was essentially a statewide independent school system, including basic educational supplies such as notebook paper, manila folders, pencils, crayons, scissors, tape, staples, and all the reading material they could get. Throughout the spring of 1964, COFO tapped into its growing network of liberal allies across America and asked them to donate supplies to the upcoming Mississippi Freedom Summer. The civil rights activists received an enormous response. Dozens of church groups, academic departments, nonprofit organizations, "Friends of SNCC" chapters, individuals, and the parents of Freedom Summer volunteers sent hundreds of boxes of school supplies, books, and magazines from every corner of the United States. Some even donated expensive educational tools such as microscopes, film projectors, or sewing machines, which gave young black students access to instruments their regular schools could never afford. The books were particularly important for Freedom School students. Because of local segregation laws, most African Americans did not have access to Mississippi's public libraries. Aside from the Bible, the only books they used were those provided by the public school system. But these texts were extremely problematic because white school officials censored schoolbooks and usually only gave African American students the tattered hand-me-down books from white schools. With the boxes of books that arrived in Mississippi that summer, Freedom School administrators were able to organize a number of "Freedom Libraries" across the state. Not all the books were new, but at least they were not censored. Access to black writers such as James Baldwin, Richard Wright, and Zora Neale Hurston generated powerful reactions among many students. Overall, the donations from external benefactors were essential to the Freedom School experience.[54]

Freedom School classes were exciting and spirited. Most schools opened each day with freedom songs to warm up for class activities and academic instruction. Many students already knew freedom songs from previous movement experiences. Those who did not know the songs learned quickly with the help of their peers and teachers. Classes began in earnest after the singing. Daily subjects varied widely among Freedom Schools, depending on the composition of teachers and students, but the curriculum at virtually every school was flexible and adjusted to meet student needs. Instructors had to teach what students wanted to learn or the voluntary schools would have sat empty all summer long. Some teachers offered remedial lessons on basic arithmetic, grammar, or technical skills. Others focused on drawing, painting, writing, or French, if that was what pupils desired. Freedom School students requested a wide variety of activities. In Holly Springs, a group of students spent time researching and writing a play based on the life of Medgar Evers. In other places, students urged teachers to allow open debates over topics such as the role of nonviolence in the movement. Debates were popular among Freedom School students. Some students travelled across town or to nearby communities to debate young people from other schools. Students relished the newfound opportunities to share their strong opinions. Former Freedom School student Anthony Harris remembered the importance of the debates in "building self-confidence that you can express yourself and you don't have to be timid."[55]

Much of what happened in those Freedom School classrooms was improvised. Classrooms became participatory democracies and flexible academic communities. Freedom School teachers facilitated discussions and introduced lessons, but students dictated much of the in-class activities. Freedom School students wrote plays and poems, read books and magazines, and helped plan future protests. They also created and embraced leadership roles, fulfilling one of the primary objectives of the Freedom School program. In the schools, they learned and grew, but out on the streets they led. Throughout Freedom Summer, students ventured into their communities to help canvass potential voters, attend mass meetings, join local marches, and conduct sit-ins. Freedom School students had a large presence in their communities and their energy and enthusiasm was inspiring to see. It is impossible to list all that they did, but many of their actions are chronicled in the essays published in this collection.[56]

Perhaps the most impressive student initiative was the organization of a Freedom School Convention, which took place in Meridian between August 7 and 9. The Freedom School Convention brought together students from across the state under the banner of the Mississippi Student Union (MSU), a short-lived youth organization composed almost entirely of Freedom School students. This type of statewide meeting had been conceived as part of the initial Freedom School plan, and in July Freedom School administrators began seriously contemplating ways to execute the idea. They called an organizational meeting in Jackson and invited several high school–age

Freedom School students to join. On July 25, a small group of student leaders from the Meridian, McComb, Columbus, and Vicksburg Freedom Schools met with older COFO activists in Jackson to finalize the convention planning. The students appreciated the advice of older activists, but refused to allow all the decisions to be made for them. At one point during the organizational meeting, the group of Freedom School students asked the older activists to leave the room so they could discuss some of the plans on their own. Roscoe Jones, one of the Freedom School students present at the meeting, recalled Freedom School Convention Chairwoman Joyce Brown of McComb telling her young colleagues, "We all have a mind. They're not going to tell us everything to do. We want to think outside the box." After the organizational meeting, Freedom School administrators told teachers that each school should select three delegates to attend the convention (some schools sent more) in Meridian, which held the largest school in the state. Meridian students, with the help of older local activists, were placed in charge of helping to secure temporary housing for convention attendees.[57]

The Mississippi Freedom School Convention opened on August 7, 1964, the night of veteran activist Dave Dennis's stirring eulogy to slain civil rights worker and Meridian native James Chaney. Upon arriving in Meridian, dozens of Freedom School student representatives attended Chaney's memorial service and joined a peaceful march in his honor. Convention activities began the following Saturday morning at 9:30. Freedom School student representatives, ranging in age from thirteen to twenty-five, met for two days, split into four committees each day to discuss specific issues facing their communities. Saturday's committees focused on public accommodations, housing, foreign affairs, and medical care. Sunday's committees concentrated on federal aid, city maintenance, job opportunities, and voter registration. Beyond the committee work, student representatives also engaged in debates, shared stories from their schools and communities, and attended speeches given by movement leaders such as Bob Moses, Staughton Lynd, and the legendary labor activist A. Philip Randolph, who was visiting Mississippi from New York. The Convention ended with attendees adopting a statewide Freedom School Convention Platform based on the conclusions of the eight committees. The platform was an ambitious and comprehensive list of demands and suggestions that the students sent to the president of the United States and a number of other influential politicians.[58]

The Freedom School Convention was a powerful moment for both students and older movement veterans. Roscoe Jones remembered the importance of "the fact that we were all together and we were together in a common cause." Just as in their individual Freedom Schools, convention attendees spent those days learning, debating, and growing. Of course, they also sang, opening each day by locking arms with their African American brothers and sisters from across the state and belting out the freedom songs that had carried each of them through the long, hot days of that life-changing summer. The convention solidified camaraderie among Freedom School students and emboldened many young leaders by exposing them to similarly engaged peers. After the convention, attendees returned to their home schools and shared the experience with their local classmates. The convention also had a major impact on older activists who were heartened by the interactions they witnessed between the student leaders. Freedom School coordinator Staughton Lynd remembered riding back to COFO headquarters with Bob Moses after the convention. Years later, Lynd still remembered Moses sitting quiet, but "aglow" in the backseat of the car, "as if what he had seen at that Freedom School Convention was the reason he was doing all that he was doing." The inspirational Freedom School students, wading with bright eyes through the cruel oppression of Mississippi Jim Crow, could always arouse older adults. The way they talked about their hopes and dreams made it clear to many veteran activists that change was indeed coming to Mississippi.[59]

The Freedom School Newspapers

Not every student was able to participate in the Freedom School Convention, but the schools allowed for nearly all of their voices to be heard. From Charles Cobb's original prospectus in the fall of 1963 to the New York City Curriculum Conference the following March, Freedom School organizers recognized the value of encouraging student expression and consistently stressed the importance of expressive critical thinking. As was explained in the original Freedom School curriculum, "The value of the Freedom Schools will derive mainly from what the teachers are able to elicit from the students in terms of comprehension and expression of their experiences."[60]

This approach was a radical change from the experiences of most Freedom School students. For generations, black Mississippi youths had been told what they *could not* say or think. Many had grown up learning ways to mask their true feelings as an essential tool of survival in the Jim Crow South. Black Mississippi youths had always felt the oppression, but few had been given the opportunity to voice their objections. By facilitating and encouraging expression, Freedom Schools fostered revolutionary approaches to critical thinking and social engagement. In Freedom Schools, civil rights activists asked young people to evaluate their society and articulate ways to change it. From those discussions emerged a wave of young people ready to engage their environments in new, remarkable ways. The students used the gift of expression to challenge the status quo in their neighborhoods, cities, state, and country. They became capable social and cultural critics empowered with the ability to challenge every aspect of their oppression. It was a powerful transformation for thousands of young people who had been told their entire lives that the finest opportunities of their society were not for them. The articles published in Freedom School newspapers capture the essence of the importance of student expression.

By mid-July, statewide Freedom School coordinator Staughton Lynd noted the existence of at least twelve school newspapers being produced by Freedom School students. While some newspaper articles included the authors' full names, others displayed only first or abbreviated names to protect writers' identities. Students of all ages wrote articles, but most authors were reportedly between the ages of thirteen and fifteen.[61]

One of the most intriguing aspects of the emergence of Freedom School newspapers was the lack of movement coverage in other Mississippi papers. Most local white-owned daily newspapers ignored movement coverage altogether. African American papers that provided movement coverage were subject to threats and economic reprisals. Because of this constant intimidation, very few Mississippi newspapers covered movement activities at all. As young people filled the void of movement journalism, the Freedom School newspapers represented an important development in the history of African Americans and civil rights coverage in the Mississippi press. Taken as a whole, these informal broadsheets more than doubled the number of pro–civil rights papers in Mississippi.[62]

Freedom School students were thrilled to have the opportunity to organize and publish their own words. As Greenwood-based teacher Judy Walborn reported, "The idea of the student newspaper is the hottest thing going. The students reacted very enthusiastically to it!!" Freedom School teachers offered assistance, but it was mainly students who developed and ran the Freedom School newspapers using the typewriters and mimeograph machines donated from across the country. A Clarksdale teacher described the exciting process of producing the local Freedom School newspaper. In a letter home, the volunteer wrote, "The place looked just like a newspaper office with people running in and out, with typewriters going, and newsprint everywhere. It was excellent experience for the kids too . . . They did most of the work and made most of the decisions." McComb teacher Ira Landess worked with students on their newspaper after regularly scheduled classes and reported, "I think the kids composed an excellent first newspaper!"[63]

The Freedom School newspapers strengthened a growing student voice in Mississippi, opening new forums of creativity to Freedom School students who wrote ardently for their school newspapers. Newspapers provided safe spaces for expression, giving the students venues where they could criticize their society, report on movement activities, communicate with each other, and express their innermost hopes and dreams. The young writers plugged their struggle into the long history of black resistance, insisting that they were building upon the foundations established by leaders such as Harriet Tubman, Frederick Douglass, Nat Turner, and Sojourner Truth. They also used the newspapers to write about their own lives, composing and publishing both heart-wrenching and inspirational poems about their present realities and future prospects. Some students used the newspapers to engage each other over the definition of freedom, constantly redefining what freedom meant and what it could be. They also challenged their peers and even older local black adults, criticizing those who they thought were not doing enough to change their societies. The determined young writers, galvanized by the Freedom School experience, could not understand why some African Americans moved so slowly or even not at all. Parents, grandparents, and community elders were all subject to critique, and many of those generational conflicts appear in the Freedom School newspapers. Some students even describe arguments with older community members. The Freedom School newspapers demonstrate the fundamental seeds of change growing in the Freedom School students. Their unbridled ambitions reverberate throughout their writings. The schools changed their lives, and students regularly used newspaper essays to offer dramatic affirmations of their personal transformations. As Bossie Mae Harring testified in the *Drew Freedom Fighter*, "[S]omeone has opened our eyes to freedom and we will walk in the light of freedom until we achieve the victory."[64]

Freedom School newspapers were distributed at businesses and churches in local black communities. Students also shared the newspapers with parents, siblings, and neighbors. There were no official distribution networks or subscription lists, but the papers made their way into the hands of local African Americans through informal exchanges. The reactions of black Mississippi adults to the young generation's newspapers are largely lost to history, but surely many of them were impressed and inspired by the young people's growth and ambition. According to one source of local lore, a poem in the McComb *Freedom's Journal* inspired adults to build and protect a new community center after the KKK bombed their original building. Regardless of distribution or readership, the power of the newspapers often rested in the sheer act of expression. For many students, the audience was an afterthought. Dozens of students loved writing for these small-scale publications and encouraged their peers to contribute. As the editors of the Meridian *Freedom Star* told potential contributors, "The FREEDOM STAR is your paper and any articles which you would like to submit for publication are welcome." Their attitude reflected the general approach of Freedom School students who always encouraged more people to attend the schools and refused to take no for an answer. As an eleven-year-old Palmer's Crossing student named Rita Mae told her peers, "I like to go to Freedom School. You would like it too. If you want to come and don't have a way, let us know." The hundreds of articles published in this collection clearly demonstrate how Freedom School students felt about the power of expression and illuminate how much they enjoyed producing their own newspapers.[65]

After Freedom Summer, Freedom School students remained on the frontlines of the desegregation movement. In the fall of 1964, Mississippi became the last state in America to desegregate its schools. In a controversial measure called the "Freedom of Choice" plan, white schools in some districts opened doors to some black students who were willing to integrate. Freedom School students were at the center of school integration efforts in several cities. In an early effort, Jackson-based Freedom School teacher Florence Howe and her student volunteers canvassed local neighborhoods trying to get parents to register their children. That autumn, eleven former Freedom School pupils were among the forty-three black students to register in the previously all-white Jackson schools. Other Freedom School students attempted to desegregate white high schools in Hattiesburg, Canton, and Meridian. Even more helped desegregate schools the following year, bravely becoming one of the few black students at several schools across the state. Freedom Schools helped prepare dozens of young people for that often harrowing experience. Former student Glenda Funchess explained the impact of Freedom Schools on her experiences with public school integration. "If it wasn't for that training that we got during the 1964 Freedom Summer project," she recounted, "I don't think that we would have been able to withstand the hostility and isolation and the humiliation that we were confronted with on a daily basis."[66]

Throughout the mid-to-late 1960s, as Jim Crow began crumbling with the Civil Rights Act of 1964 and the Voting Rights Act of 1965, Freedom School students remained active across the state. Young black Mississippians boycotted schools for better resources or to protest unfair educational policy or racially motivated disciplinary measures. These types of protests developed into a major freedom movement initiative among young black Mississippi students. One of the first boycotts occurred at Shaw High School in early August 1964 and helped set the tone for student activity during the upcoming year. Led by the local Mississippi Student Union (MSU), Shaw students organized a school boycott to protest local educational inequalities and demand better resources for their school. The boycott was approximately 75 percent effective, and boycotting students were able to attend the Shaw Freedom School well into the school year. The next major boycott occurred in Sharkey and Issaquena counties, which students organized in January of 1965. The boycott was sparked when black students began wearing SNCC buttons to school and refused to take them off. The school's black principal, following the instructions of an all-white school board, subsequently expelled them. Over three hundred students decided to boycott the school in sympathy. Some stayed out until the following school year altogether. During the Issaquena and Sharkey county boycotts, organizers continued offering Freedom School classes as alternatives to the counties' regular public schools.[67] The boycott inspired further action across the state. Students attending the Indianola public schools boycotted in support of the Sharkey and Issaquena county students. In Indianola alone, approximately two thousand students stayed at home. Many Freedom School veterans were among the boycotters, and a lot of their efforts were organized by the youth-run MSU, which declared that "Negroes are fed up with inferior schools, extreme brutality by the police, and similar discrimination. We're doing something about it." The brutality referred to the arrest of fifty-three protestors in Indianola and the police force's use of billy clubs and cattle prods to break up the demonstration.[68]

Across the state, politically charged students, many of whom attended or were influenced by Freedom Schools, shared stories of admirable resistance through connections facilitated by the Meridian convention. Forty-five students in Philadelphia carried forward the push for political equality when they fashioned SNCC "One Man, One Vote" buttons and defiantly wore them in school despite threats of expulsion. Students in Rolling Fork were similarly sent home for wearing freedom pins. Students in Panola County petitioned the school board to request an improvement of school facilities and threatened to boycott if their demands were not met. Valley View students protested the firing of an African American bus driver. Resistance to racially inferior education took many forms. A Jackson student was expelled for continuing to sing freedom songs in the building. In Holmes County, a principal expelled two students for singing freedom songs during the lunch period. Another principal in Starkville expelled a student for distributing an MSU petition.[69] Across the state of Mississippi, students organized, demanded better resources and treatment, and forced school authorities to listen to their requests. The spirit of Freedom Schools guided much of the activism and resistance. Even if the young protestors had not attended the schools themselves, most had been affected by Freedom School students who had returned to their normal schools after the Freedom Summer to lead their peers.

Freedom Schools Today

Since 1964, the Mississippi Freedom Schools have served as a powerful institutional model rooted in the finest examples of American educational activism. As early as the fall of 1964, Freedom School administrators began receiving hundreds of letters asking for materials that would help other groups replicate the Mississippi Freedom School model. More than fifty years after Freedom Summer, their influence extends across the United States. Many contemporary educational institutions cite those 1964 Freedom Schools as important predecessors to their modern policies, programs, and tactics. The most visible of these are the vast numbers of Freedom Schools conducted by the Children's Defense Fund (CDF). Marian Wright Edelman, a civil rights activist and the first African American admitted to the Mississippi State Bar Association, established the CDF in 1973 to help challenge "the United States to raise its standards by improving policies and programs for children."[70] Edelman's organization is especially interested in helping children from disadvantaged communities. One of the CDF's most visible activities is its modern Freedom School program. Conducted every summer in more than eighty cities across America, the CDF Freedom Schools seek to provide "summer and after-school enrichment that helps children fall in love with reading, increases their self-esteem, and generates more positive attitudes toward learning." Since 1995, the CDF Freedom School teachers have reached more than seventy thousand students and their families. Over seven thousand college students, two thousand high school students, and fifteen hundred adult site coordinators and project directors have been trained to work in Freedom Schools, some of which operate in the same Mississippi cities that first hosted Freedom Schools in 1964.[71] Students in today's Mississippi Freedom Schools are socially active just like many of the youths who came to schools fifty years before. They encourage local communities to register to vote, organize community activities, and constantly help challenge undemocratic practices in society.

Today's Freedom School teachers also go through training that teaches them many of the same principles of the original Mississippi Freedom Schools. Contemporary CDF Freedom School teachers must apply and be selected among competitive fields of applicants to work with the schools. Those accepted are invited to participate in the Ella Baker Child Policy Training Institute, a national training workshop held each year at the historic CDF Haley Farm in Clinton, Tennessee, and at the University of Tennessee–Knoxville. Unlike the mostly white 1964 Freedom Summer volunteers, most teachers hired to work in today's Children's Defense Fund Freedom Schools are African American and share a similar racial background with the scholars they teach.[72] The change in the composition of Freedom School teachers is an important development that addressed some of the racial considerations of the mid-1960s. Teachers who are drawn from the community and adopt a culturally relevant pedagogy are important factors in successful education. The teachers in the 1964 schools were from vastly different communities than those of their students in terms of geography, race, and financial status. There are some other differences, especially in the Freedom Schools' curriculum and pedagogy. The modern CDF Freedom Schools are much more institutionalized than the 1964 Mississippi ones. They have permanent funding sources, take attendance, closely measure success, and embrace a cultural awareness and cultural sensitivity in a way that closely mirrors Gloria Ladson-Billings's concept of "culturally relevant teaching."[73]

Despite the differences between historical and contemporary Freedom Schools, the programs have a similar goal. An important legacy drives their mission. Modern CDF Freedom Schools attempt to engage students through a student-centered curriculum and pedagogical approach that focuses on issues relevant to their communities, much like the Freedom Schools of 1964. The model is still attracting students, parents, and educators. The CDF Freedom School program is constantly growing and currently attracts nearly twelve thousand students each year. The CDF Freedom Schools are widespread and important. They are also not alone.

The term "Freedom School" is widely used today by educational activists across the country. Other educationally progressive institutions such as the Philadelphia Freedom Schools offer on-site tutoring and mentoring programs, distinct from the CDF, but similarly exemplifying the Freedom School legacy. The Black Radical Congress in Detroit, for instance, embraced educational and political approaches modeled after the Freedom Schools. Contemporary examples include the Chicago and Philadelphia Freedom School systems and the San Francisco Freedom School. Many of these contemporary institutions cite the influence of the 1964 Freedom Schools in their mission statements and similarly address citizenship, civil rights, and political education. Other schools continue to use the name in reference only. Today's organizers are still pursuing the dream of a more inclusive and equal democracy and incorporating students, families, and communities in the process of liberation.

Bob Moses, the pioneering civil rights activist who helped lead SNCC into Mississippi, is currently running an educational program that also embodies many elements of the Freedom School ideology. The Algebra Project, founded by Moses in 1990, is based on the community-organizing component of the Civil Rights Movement. Moses continues to make a strong connection between the movement and education, drawing direct parallels between those early days in Mississippi and the struggles that remain for today's underprivileged populations. "The most urgent social issue affecting poor people and people of color is economic access," explains Moses. "In today's world, economic access and full citizenship depend crucially on math and science literacy. I believe that the absence of math literacy in urban and rural communities throughout this country is an issue as urgent as the lack of registered Black voters in Mississippi was in 1961."[74]

In the 1990s, Bob Moses created the Algebra Project based on the idea that mathematical literacy was crucial for success in the twenty-first century. Overlooking or denying this crucial form of literacy, as is common practice in disadvantaged schools, violates the civil rights of all students. Like the organizational predecessors before it, the Algebra Project utilizes education as an organizing tool. Algebra is the point of entry into a larger struggle that not only advocates for mathematical literacy in a culturally responsive way at all levels of school, but also for changes in resource distribution, the fair treatment of all students, and equitable school policies. Moses currently helps organize branches of the Algebra Project across the United States. But in classic Highlander style, he does not simply tell communities what to do. Rather, he organizes them by asking questions and placing the opportunity for providing answers on local community members and young people. Moses and his organization help, but the onus of implementation ultimately falls on students and local communities. The Algebra Project and its attendant organization, the Young People's Project, harness the grassroots organization legacy of the Freedom Schools and embody the radical, transformative goals of education embodied by the 1964 Mississippi Freedom Schools.

As with the 1964 Freedom Schools, the actual number of current students involved with the Algebra Project is hard to gauge, but its impact has been profound and inspirational. In Jackson, Bob Moses's own daughters have helped lead an effort at Brinkley High School to challenge their students to conceptualize math in their own terms.[75] Here students engage with the past to develop a mathematical literacy needed for economic success. The Baltimore, Maryland, branch of the Algebra Project also particularly resonates with the grassroots organizing, nonviolent ethos, and political consciousness of the Civil Rights Movement. Young students run the Baltimore Algebra Project and have also participated in nonviolent protests, marches, and demonstrations aimed at raising money and resources for the city's failing public schools and disrupting the state of Maryland's plans to build a new juvenile detention center. The students occupied the center's planned site to protest the institution that was designed to house youths under the age of eighteen who had been tried as adults. Police made several arrests, sending to jail new waves of young people who dared hold the front lines of grassroots protests.[76]

Bob Moses's work also indicates a shift in civil rights education at a larger policy level. Moses reconnected two themes, the Civil Rights Movement and educational policy, in important ways that offer significant implications. The Algebra Project is indicative of the directions the freedom movement has taken and symbolizes future possibilities. Whereas 1950s and 1960s–era activism succeeded in securing a great deal of civil, political, and economic rights, today's activists like Moses have been arguing, lobbying, and organizing for education to also be considered a fundamental right guaranteed by the Constitution. Moses served on the coordinating committee for Quality Education as a Constitutional Right (QECR), a national organization that seeks to build community and political support for a constitutional amendment for quality education. In this way, education has been shaped and grounded in Civil Rights Movement principles, not only because it works to amend federal policy, but because it works to use education as a way to ensure nationwide civil rights for all children.

Another powerful example of contemporary educational activism comes from McComb, Mississippi, which hosted a Freedom

School of its own in 1964. Recently, a small group of students from McComb High School organized a commemoration of the fiftieth anniversary of the Burgland High School walkout of 1961, an important movement moment that was largely unrecognized until the young people began advocating for a tribute. In 2011, students at McComb High School organized a chapter of the Young People's Project to develop a remembrance service for the walkout and produce a documentary detailing the historic event. The group's documentary won four awards at the Mississippi History Day competition and earned several young students a trip to National History Day in Washington, D.C., where their documentary was very well received. Today, students from the McComb School District work with local community members to run a blog called "McComb Legacies" that commemorates the important history of the McComb freedom struggle and provides updates on current McComb student projects. Their important work also includes developing a "Local Cultures" course in the public school curriculum, which they developed in response to Mississippi House Bill 2718—a bill passed in 2008 that incorporates Civil Rights Movement history into the state's social studies curriculum. In addition to their community engagement and commemorating important milestones, local McComb students have also advocated for a progressive educational agenda that includes sex education to combat the rise of pregnancy and sexually transmitted infections. They also address issues such as parenting.[77] These students are organizing on their own to achieve a quality education and use history as a way to engage and improve their communities.

Sadly, the fight for educational equality, an epic struggle throughout the American past, remains an unfulfilled promise. Especially in the era of "No Child Left Behind," frustrated educators, policy makers, parents, and scholars have sometimes looked to the democratic idealism expressed in educational programs such as the Mississippi Freedom Schools for historical lessons in addressing contemporary educational problems. The problems addressed by such schools stem from debates over community control and racialized issues such as the achievement gap, racial tracking, and resegregation. Today's schools have become highly segregated both in and out of the South, a troubling reality that warrants further critical examination of educational reform in the post-*Brown* era. Nonetheless, the lessons of freedom in terms of classroom pedagogy and educational policy learned in the 1964 Mississippi Freedom Schools can still inform contemporary educational practices as today's activists continue fighting to fulfill the unfinished educational promises of the black freedom struggle.

Conclusion

This collection contains Freedom School newspapers gathered from archives, libraries, and personal collections across America. Because Freedom Summer volunteers arrived from all corners of the United States (and some even beyond), their personal papers are now spread in archives across the nation. Surely, the newspapers also exist elsewhere, in attics and basements in Mississippi and other scattered personal collections, but most of the ones published here came from libraries that hold significant Freedom Summer–related collections—especially the State Historical Society of Wisconsin in Madison, Wisconsin, the McCain Library and Archives in Hattiesburg, Mississippi, and the King Library and Archives in Atlanta, Georgia—and a half-dozen other archives that hold smaller civil rights–document collections. Several newspapers were donated by former Freedom School teachers who kept them through the years and we are thankful for their generosity. Some of the newspapers are actually quite rare and difficult to find. Some were scattered through separate ollections. Page one might have been in one place with page two located elsewhere. For example, parts of the Meridian *Freedom Star* were discovered years apart in Atlanta and New York. Collecting these newspapers was a time-consuming but incredibly rewarding task. It is our hope that this collection can make a small contribution to the original mission of the Freedom School project and also offer some use for today's students, teachers, and activists interested in examining the Mississippi Freedom Schools as models for social change.

To the best of our knowledge, all the newspapers published in this book were produced by Freedom School students during the summer of 1964. Several other civil rights–era community newspapers and black middle- and high-school newspapers did exist. Many communities started producing civil rights papers shortly after Freedom Summer or continued publishing issues of the newspapers started by Freedom School students. In several cases, Freedom School newspapers were taken over by older activists and became more sophisticated community newsletters. The newspapers published here were selected because they were definitively produced by the Freedom School students during the summer of 1964. All available evidence shows that Freedom School students, with the help of their teachers and other local community members, ran the newspapers and wrote the articles themselves. This book does contain two noted examples of older activists writing articles for the newspapers (a brief list written by a Freedom School teacher and another letter written by an older McComb activist), but the rest of the words seen and transcribed verbatim here were written by black Mississippi youths. Their perspectives, which are often missing in histories of the movement, are incredibly important.

The Civil Rights Movement is usually understood, taught, and remembered through the lens of its most famous leaders and their struggle to eliminate racial segregation in public spaces. The Montgomery Bus Boycott, the Sit-In Movement of 1960, and the Freedom Rides were all examples of direct-action desegregation efforts, often celebrated through iconic leaders such as Rosa Parks, Dr. Martin Luther King Jr., and Ralph Abernathy. These are, of course, important moments that offer powerful lessons. This volume adds another dimension to that already powerful movement history by showing how young, everyday black students in middle and high schools across Mississippi experienced the dramatic racial transformations taking place all around them. Their perspectives have been largely overshadowed by dozens of books that analyze the speeches and rhetoric of leaders such as Dr. Martin Luther King Jr. and Malcolm X.

This collection provides its readers with an important glimpse into the ways young people responded to both Jim Crow and the

Civil Rights Movement. It also helps push the understanding of the movement beyond desegregation and direct action demonstrations. The Freedom School students talk about desegregating busses, lunch counters, public schools, and a host of other spaces, but they also talk about the intellectual liberation provided by attending Freedom Schools and joining the movement. For these young black students, Freedom Schools meant so much more than basic learning processes. The schools were also incredible avenues for intellectual liberation. As one student wrote, Freedom Schools were like "having the lights turned on after you have lived all your life in a darkened room." The newspapers in this collection offer a glimpse of those transformations. Through the articles, essays, stories, and poems printed here, one can see how those young people revolted against everything that Jim Crow society had tried to teach them. They resisted not just with their actions, but also with their words, writing letters and commentaries to their broader society, demanding freedom and resolving to never settle for second-class citizenship. For many young people especially, the movement's greatest transformations occurred not in broader society but in their hearts and minds.[78]

Historians, educators, activists, students, and all those connected to American education should find this book useful as a teaching and/or research tool as they strive to advance their own interests and goals. For historians of the American South and the Civil Rights Movement, this collection offers an extensive set of previously uncollected primary source material that can serve as an invaluable research aid or a rich set of documents for students of American history. For elementary, middle, and high school social studies and English teachers, this material can be easily aligned with content standards that address twentieth century American history, multiple perspectives in American history, and alternative uses of media during the Civil Rights Movement of the 1960s. The voices of African American youth who confronted Jim Crow and legal segregation offer a genuinely alternative perspective to traditional textbooks that cover the history of the Civil Rights Movement. This primary source collection also provides teachers with a convenient opportunity to enact culturally relevant and multicultural education to meet the interests and needs of a diverse student population. Most importantly, this collection offers students a snapshot into the lives, hopes, and ambitions of a generation of students that can still inform the struggle of young people today, over fifty years after the historic summer of 1964.

The writings of Freedom School students are collected in the newspapers that follow. They are heartwarming and inspirational as much as they are informative. We cannot fully anticipate the broad and creative ways that readers will understand and use this powerful collection. But we encourage audiences to use these documents in creative ways that consider the Freedom School students and their legacy within the broader history of the struggle for black education. It is our hope that a wide range of inter-disciplinary scholars, teachers, and activists will be informed and inspired by these writings. But perhaps the greatest potential audience for this collection is today's young people. This book offers contemporary youths a unique opportunity to learn about the Civil Rights Movement from the perspectives of people their own age and connect it to their lives today. As much as the Civil Rights Movement accomplished, the struggle for access to quality education continues. It is hoped that this volume will increase young people's appreciation of how the movement impacted people their own age and reinforce for them the importance of learning and the tremendous power of education as they pursue their own dreams.

Benton County Freedom Train

Benton County is a quiet and rural area of northern Mississippi. Although it was not known as a hotbed of civil rights activism, local African Americans participated in the NAACP and the Citizen's League, a small clandestine group of men that attempted to register and organize black voters. The mass meetings that defined the Benton County movement often took place at St. James Church, a popular meeting space for locals during the Freedom Summer. Students in Benton County were influenced by civil rights activities in Holly Springs, located just twenty miles away. The Benton County Freedom School was established just a couple of weeks into Freedom Summer after locals heard about the Holly Springs and other Mississippi Freedom Schools. In this issue of the local Freedom School newspaper, black students in Benton County react to the freshly minted Civil Rights Act of 1964, which promised full equality to the young students. The students in this issue also discuss the role of black and white students working together in desegregated schools. After Freedom Summer, other local African Americans started writing for the Benton County Freedom Train, which published regular issues until 1968.

News Bulletin: Civil Rights Bill
by Henry Reaves

Now the civil rights bill has passed at last. You had better exercise your rights and exercise them fast, or the Negro will be in the same condition as he was in the past.

How We Live in Mississippi
by Mary Francie Harris

At the beginning of March our father begins to break land. He has to break the land sometimes with tractors and mules. The

Masthead of the *Benton County Freedom Train*.
Courtesy of the Wisconsin Historical Society.

men work hard all day long from seven o'clock until twelve o'clock when they stop for dinner; then back to the field at one o'clock until six o'clock, and come home and eat and go to bed. That's how it is until they get ready to plant cotton.

Then when the cotton is up and ready to chop, we chop most of the time until summer school begins. The school opens in July, and we go to school.

But now it is different from the past few years. It has been hard for all of us, but this year the people from all over the United States have come to help us. All we can say is we want freedom; everybody wants freedom. So, people, lift up your head and let your light shine. Let's begin to act like human beings. To the workers who are here to help us, I can say that we all love you, but God loves you best.

How Negroes Earn Their Living in Mississippi
by Shirley J. Richard

Most Negroes earn their living by farming. Some have as many as 60 acres, others have five, ten, 30, etc. You don't find any Negroes with as many acres of cotton as whites.

The average person gets paid by the hour. We work eight to nine hours each day and are paid daily after work is over. We get only $3.00 per day. In Michigan City, Mississippi, Negroes are paid only $2.50, and they chop cotton eight and one-half and nine hours each day.

The work that we do is rough. The men whom we work for is responsible for having fresh cold water handy in the field for the workers to drink. The white owners fail to bring enough water for each person to drink. The whites also fail to take us to the store in time to eat dinner.

We are treated very badly by the whites. We are called names; when they are handing things to us they throw it to us or drop it for fun. When a Negro is walking down the street or roadside, whites pass hollerin; "nigger" or "black". When we are working in the fields, the whites say, "Go to work, nigger."

For the women or girls, white women hire them to house clean or babysit for a low price of $2.00 and $3.50 a day. We get very little for such a lot of work, such as: ironing, washing clothes, washing windows, cooking three meals each day, cutting grass, scrubbing floors, and other things. Many walk to and from work. They also work eight to nine hours a day.

When it's harvest, Negroes pick cotton by hand at $2.00 for a hundred pounds and some places $3.00 per hundred. The white man pays the Negro what he thinks he needs without showing him the record of how much each is supposed to get. Many Negroes live on a white man's place where they sharecrop, half and half, and rent. What we owe for cotton seeds are taken out of our half of the money. When we are finished paying our debts, we have only $500.00 and sometimes less.

This is the average way of a Negro's life in Mississippi. Of course all Negroes don't live on a white man's place. Some Negroes have their own place to live on. Some Negroes work for other Negroes as for the Whites. Some Whites help Negroes by lending them small amounts of money, as $20 and $30 for a while. So this is the average Negro's way of living.

Social Life
by Chyleen Matthews

To be social, you sit down and relax and enjoy yourself with other people and serve refreshments, watch T.V., or listen to the radio. Sometimes you sit down and talk or go swimming and have pictures made. I think that most of the girls would rather have a party or a picnic and go on a ride for the best social activities.

But the boys like to hunt and go on hikes. When you go on a picnic or a party you should not eat too much because it will make you sick; but some people don't know when they get enough.

The Negroes and Whites
by Archie B. Richard

We as Negroes should be thankful for these nice people who have come over from Washington, New York, Chicago, and these different cities to help us, for we know as Negroes that we have had our share of hard times. While we are working for Whites—ironing, housecleaning, etc.—we can't even go into cafes, or go swimming. And no matter how hard we work for them, we sometimes are told to go to backdoors of Whites. Think of how poor the times our forefathers had in slavery days. After so many years of hard work for the Negroes, the president, Abraham Lincoln, thought that the Negroes should have freedom like Whites in the year 1863. No more slavery, but still just because our skins are dark, I wonder why they got the idea we are lower than they.

"All men are created equal." That statement means a lot. The Bible says, "Let us love one another and live together, for we are all children of God." We should think of what these statements mean.

We have been treated badly so long by the Whites, it's time someone made a change about this situation. But as we know, no job can be done without the help of the Lord. We need him at work or play—everything we do. And I really believe in my heart it's the love and will of God that what these civil rights people are trying to do was his fixing.

So many times we have to go to windows of cafes while Whites go inside. We go to stores and are there first, but then Whites come in and are waited on first. Or we may be walking alone minding our own business and whites come along and meddle, or maybe throw something or yell at you. And nothing can be done, for as soon as Negroes would do that to Whites, the law is ready to put you in jail or something of that kind. We are getting tired. But God sees what we have to go through, and that's why he has sent people around to change this law so we, too, can have a fair chance.

Now that the civil rights bill have been signed, we children going to school have a better chance of learning the different subjects we wish to, if we put our minds to it. We can finish school, go to college, and make a new start in life: find good jobs, make maybe more than $3.00 a day. We hope and pray that everything works out okay that we all can work and play together—Whites and Negroes—in the name of the Lord.

We pray to God to watch over the civil rights people in Mississippi, that nothing happens to them while they're trying to help us.

The Negroes of Mississippi
by Dorothy Jean Richard

There are many Negroes in Mississippi and their jobs are mostly of farming. Some are maids and they make from $2.50 to $3.50

while working from 8:00 to 5:00. Usually their wages are no higher than $3.50.

Cotton Chopping Time: this time some people were paid from $2.50 to $3.00. Last year the people were paid $3.50 for 100 pounds, but this year at the place where I worked, the people were paid $3.00. Working hours in the cotton field are from 6:00am to 12:00 noon and then they go back at 1:00 o'clock and chop to 6:00pm. Usually, those who get $3.00 go to the field at 7 o'clock, stop at 11:30 for lunch and go back to the field at 1 o'clock and stop at 5 o'clock in the evening. We much prefer to stop at 5 o'clock. When picking cotton time comes the majority of the people start from $2.50 a hundred for chopping cotton and then finally they go up to $3.00 and $3.50. Later on in the fall they may make as much as $3.75 a hundred.

I am very glad that someone has to come help us. I hope it won't be any more trouble. It's a terrible thing to have your friends missing. The only thing I can think of is death. I am sorry about that.

The Mount Zion CME Church
by Willie Thomas Matthews

The Mount Zion CME Church in Ashland, Mississippi had a Fathers' Day program which was a great success. The entrie [*sic*] afternoon was dedicated to the fathers under the leadership of Rev. Luther Miner. The program included, amongst other things, a welcome address given by Willie Thomas Matthews.

The Three Who Are Missing
by Walter Thomas Rooks

How do the Whites feel about the three who are missing? They do not feel anything. You Negroes feel sorry, but the White is not thinking about it, about the three who are missing. You know about it.

You have all heard about it and you all know about it. I think the laws are not working as well as they should. Do you think so? I think so and so the Whites are not doing the best they can, but they are doing what they please. Well, that's how I feel about the three who are missing.

Why I Like to Go to School
by Gloria Joan Winston

I like to go to school because I am very interested in learning different things. Education is very important. For example, you have to have an education in order to get a decent job.

I like all subjects, but my favorite subject is Science. I like Science because it teaches me about the out-of-doors, about the earth that surrounds us, of the universe, and about the plants and animals. For example, Science teaches us the many uses of plants and animals. We got some of our food from plants as well as clothing, wool, and rubber. Some plants are good for animals and they use these plants for food while other plants are harmful. I also learned that we are dependent on animals just as we are dependent on plants. From animals we get clothing, food, and other products. Animals are also useful for farming, transportation, and other work. Animals have even more uses. Some animals are pets and friends.

School is very enjoyable for me mostly because of Science.

Feelings about the Freedom Workers
by Alice Ann Judge

Questions were asked about how we Negroes feel about the freedom workers coming into Mississippi. Some of the Negroes are not pleased. Most of the Whites are not pleased. They do not want the Negroes to vote for their freedom. They do not want the Negroes to have good-paying jobs. Almost all of the white people are against the freedom workers. For this I am very sorry and very hurt and I am sure others are too. I hope so.

When I heard about the three freedom workers being missing I thought to myself that I do not want to believe that they are dead—burned. I don't want to think though I wish they would be found.

I hope we do get our freedom. Most Negroes earn their living by cotton while the white man gets all of the office jobs. The left over jobs are given to the Negroes. For example, Negroes make very little money, no more than $3.00 or $4.00 in the cotton fields. All men should have the same chance. If we Negroes get the chance to vote then we will have the same chances as the white man.

The Things I Do
by Anna Lee Stinson

I live in Holly Springs Mississippi. I go to W. T. Sims High School. The first thing I do when I get home from school is my homework. Sometimes I don't feel like it, but sometimes it is fun. When I get my homework done I begin to do the dishes. Sometimes my sister helps, but I like to do it myself because she can get in the way.

My father works at the Old Brick Kiln in Holly Springs. My mother stays at home and takes care of the baby. When school is out we pick cotton. We get $3.00 a hundred pounds for picking cotton. And those are the things we do.

Working Together
by James Rooks

I think that the freedom workers are doing a great job of teaching. I think that the Whites and Negroes out to pull together and work together with one another. Both Negroes and whites should work together and farm together. It certainly would make a real nice world.

My Morning Routine
by Larry Price

The first thing I do in the morning is get up and say my prayers. Then I go to the bathroom, take a bath, brush my teeth, comb my hair, and dress. The next thing I do is eat my breakfast. I then feed the chickens and make by [*sic*] bed. After that I wait for the school bus to arrive.

We Shall Overcome!

20 July 64 - A Paper for All who want their Freedom and Full Equality Now.

DREW FREEDOM FIGHTER

In spite of 7 arrests during the mass meeting on Tuesday, June 14, the mass meeting on Wednesday night was even larger. The people seemed even more determined to work for their freedom. The policeworo not scaring the people of Drew any more. This was proved by what happened Wednesday night!

The Wednesday meeting started on the outside of the Holly Grove Church. The question to start with is, why couldn't it be held inside? The next question is, what made the deacons of the church decide that we couldn't even meet outside their church? When the deacon said that we could not meet on church property, the mass meeting moved next door, to an empty lot. The people were singing about Freedom. Charles MacLaurin was talking about how to achieve Freedom Now.

Then the police came with the owner of the empty lot, and the owner said we could not meet on her empty lot. The people voted to continue the meeting by going into the street. So about 60 people took the step for freedom, and followed Charles MacLaurin into the street. Twenty-five people were arrested. The charge was blocking the sidewalk. But the people were not afraid of jail. The police had to turn some of them away and told them that they could not be arrested. The people who went to jail went singing, and the people outside the walls of the Drew City Jail, could hear Charles MacLaurin still talking about Freedom inside the jail.

Jail was not pleasant. Lice and roaches and a snake and little air and the smell of urine. But they were not ashamed to be in jail. They had gone to jail for their freedom. Ten citizens of Drew went with 6 citizens of Ruleville and 2 COFO workers. There will be more mass meetings, and even more people will come. There may be more arrests, as the police and the mayor of Drew see their society crumbling. But we will never never turn back.

THE FIGHT FOR FREEDOM
by Bessie Mae Herring
I think the Negro freedom workers and the white workers have made a very good start, and by the help of God we shall overcome some day. The Negro people have been a stepping stone for the white people all their lives because they didn't know better. But someone has opened our eyes to freedom and we will walk in the light of freedom until we achieve the victory.

FROM THE RULEVILLE STUDENT ACTION GROUP by Ora Doss
The teachers at Ruleville Central High School do not take any part in the registration program when we try to talk to them. Some of them showinterest but others do not. We will put forth every effort to change them because how can they teach us howto be first class citizens when they are not citizens themselves. Something that the Student Action Group might do in order to inform the teachers of the necessity to become first class citizens is picket the school or have a school walk-out.

Masthead of the *Drew Freedom Fighter*.
Courtesy of the Wisconsin Historical Society.

Drew Freedom Fighter

Located in Sunflower County and just across the border from Bolivar County, Drew Freedom School had students who came of age in one of the busiest movement centers in the state. Legendary African American activists such as Fannie Lou Hamer and Amzie Moore lived within a dozen miles of their hometowns and helped generate a lot of local activity. Drew Freedom School students published the Drew Freedom Fighter shortly after their school first opened on July 6, 1964. Like thousands of others across Mississippi, young black students in Drew were interested in going to Freedom School and enrolled enthusiastically. The students were also galvanized by the dedication and courage of veteran civil rights activists and Freedom Summer volunteers who were regularly arrested throughout the summer. One such activist, Charles McLaurin, a SNCC organizer in the Delta country, gave stirring speeches from inside the Drew jailhouse. Students were captivated and emboldened by the examples set by older activists. As one young journalist reported in the Freedom Fighter, "The police were not scaring the people of Drew any more." With dedicated teachers and determined Freedom School students, Drew remained an important part of the 1964 Freedom Summer campaign. In 1971, the small Delta town gained national notoriety when a twenty-five-year-old white man named Wesley Parks shot and killed eighteen-year-old African American student Jo Etha Collier on the night that she graduated with honors from the recently desegregated Drew High School.

In spite of 7 arrests during the mass meeting on Tuesday, June 14, the mass meeting on Wednesday night was even larger. The people seemed even more determined to work for their freedom. The police were not scaring the people of Drew any more. This was proved by what happened Wednesday night:

The Wednesday meeting started on the outside of the Holly Grove Church. The question to start with is, why couldn't it be held inside? The next question is, what made the deacons of the church decide that we couldn't even meet <u>outside</u> their church? When the deacon said that we could not meet on church property, the mass meeting moved next door, to an empty lot. The people were singing about Freedom. Charles MacLaurin was talking about how to achieve Freedom Now.

Then the police came with the owner of the empty lot, and the owner said we could not meet on her empty lot. The people voted to continue the meeting by going into the street. So about 60 people took the step for freedom, and followed Charles MacLaurin into the street. Twenty-five people were arrested. The charge was blocking the sidewalk. But the people were not afraid of jail. The police had to turn some of them away and tell them that they could not be arrested. The people who went to jail went singing, and the people outside the walls of the Drew City Jail could hear Charles MacLaurin still talking about Freedom inside the jail.

Jail was not pleasant. Lice and roaches and a snake and little air and the smell of urine. But they were not ashamed to be in jail. They had gone to jail for their freedom. The citizens of Drew went with the 6 citizens of Ruleville and 9 COFO workers. There will be more mass meetings, and even more people will come. They may be more arrests, as the police and the mayor of Drew see their society crumbling. But we will never never turn back.

The Fight for Freedom
By Bossie Mae Harring

I think the Negro freedom workers and the white workers have made a very good start, and by the help of God we shall overcome one day. The Negro people have been a stepping stone for the white people all their lives because they didn't know better. But someone has opened our eyes to freedom and we will walk in the light of freedom until we achieve the victory.

From the Ruleville Student Action Group
By Ora Boss

The teachers at Ruleville Central High School do not take any part in the registration program when we try to talk to them.

Some of them show interest but others do not. We will put forth every effort to change them because how can they teach us how to be first class citizens when they are not citizens themselves. Something that the Student Action Group might do in order to inform the teachers of the necessity to become first class citizens is picket the school or have a school walk-out.

Vote Freedom Democrat

The big, old, political party of Mississippi is the segregated Democratic Party. This party is owned and operated by white people like James Eastland and T. A. Fleming. These white people don't know what the Negro people want. They don't even care about Negro people.

We want a party in Mississippi that is integrated not segregated. We want a party that will make the boss man on the plantation pay more than $3 a day. We want a party here in Mississippi that will give us responsible policemen and good mayors—not policemen that beat people and throw them into jail for nothing and not mayors who sit in their offices and get fat and care only about white people.

We will call this new party the Freedom Democratic Party. It will be the best party in Mississippi, because it will be owned and operated by Negro and white people together. People all over the United States and all over the world will hear about this party, because it will stand for freedom and justice for <u>all</u> people in Mississippi.

In August all the Democratic parties of all 50 states of the United States will have a meeting. Will the <u>Freedom</u> Democratic Party of Mississippi be at the meeting or will the same old <u>segregated</u> Democratic party be there? All the Negro people should sign the Freedom Registration form. The <u>Freedom</u> Democratic party will win. And the old segregated Democratic party will have to <u>step aside.</u>

The <u>Freedom</u> Democratic Party will hold the meetings all over the Sunflower County. It will hold meetings all over Mississippi. It will elect people to go to a County Meeting. It will elect some people to go to a state meeting. This party fights for freedom of the Negro people. Everyone should attend local meetings of this party. We must work for freedom. No change comes unless people <u>work</u> for a change.

The Booker T. Washington and W. E. B. Du Bois Argument: A Dialogue

<u>Scene:</u> Du Bois and Washington meet at a convention. Du Bois is a short man, with a keen-looking face and sharp eyes. Washington is tall, well dressed, and well-to-do-looking.

<u>Du Bois</u> (clearing his throat): Good evening, Sir.

<u>Booker T. Washington</u> (looking hard at him): Good evening.

<u>Du Bois:</u> I heard the speech you made about segregation. You really do believe in that segregation.

<u>Washington:</u> Yes, I do believe in segregation.

<u>Du Bois:</u> Why?

<u>Washington:</u> Well, you know how white and colored can't get along together.

<u>Du Bois:</u> They can get along together if we lazy Negroes wake up, and start doing something for ourselves!

<u>Washington:</u> Why, you integrationist you!

<u>Du Bois:</u> I want to see our race with better educations and finer homes. I don't want to see them treated like slaves, living in homes that are nothing but nasty lumber thrown together! I want to see Negroes voting like citizens.

<u>Washington:</u> Let's stop talking about the vote and higher education. I'm sick of that!

<u>Du Bois:</u> You're just an old fool so mixed up in segregation, you don't know what the word integration means.

<u>Washington</u> (getting madder): How in the world do you think you're going to get the two races together.

<u>Du Bois:</u> By getting all the Negroes together fighting for integration.

<u>Washington:</u> Fighting! And getting the living daylight beat out of you.

<u>Du Bois:</u> Good bye, Mr. Washington!!!

<u>Washington:</u> Good bye Dr. Du Bois!!!

Violence in Harlem—New York City (the <u>New York Times</u>)

Harlem, and places like Harlem all over the North, are the ghettos where Negroes live in big Northern Cities. The people there are tired of overcrowding, overcharging, and police brutality. The riots of the past few days started out not to be riots; the people from CORE only wanted to demonstrate against a recent terrible case of police brutality. But, unfortunately, terribly, there was a great deal of violence. You can understand some of the feelings of the police, and of the people of Harlem:

"Go home, go home," a sweating red-faced Captain shouted through a bullhorn.

A sermon came back from a man in the mob: "We are home, baby."

The Freedom Carrier (Greenwood, MS)

*The Greenwood movement began in earnest during the summer of
1962 when Cleveland, Mississippi, native Sam Block began organizing the local black community, knocking on doors and trying to recruit
African American residents to attend mass meetings. Slowly but surely,
Block and other SNCC workers connected with local African Americans
including Cleveland Jordan, Aaron Johnson, Robert Burns, and Jerry
Chestnut, who helped develop a network of local people who were willing to try and register to vote. They worked with newly recruited local
African American residents to establish Citizenship Schools and a local
library to help teach black Greenwood residents how to complete registration forms. These voter registration efforts in Greenwood helped lead
to the Freedom Vote in the fall of 1963, a statewide mock-voter registration campaign that laid the foundation for the independent Mississippi
Freedom Democratic Party (MFDP).*

*Civil rights activists working in Greenwood always encountered
severe resistance. Through the local Citizens' Council, white segregationists used economic intimidation to punish and threaten local black
residents who participated in the Civil Rights Movement. African
Americans could potentially lose their jobs or even homes for joining
the movement, leading to many difficult decisions including one that
resulted in the eviction of SNCC activist Sam Block from a black-owned
boardinghouse. Local white supremacists also used violence to quell
movement activities. During the Freedom Vote drive in 1963, Greenwood
police used dogs to control and pacify peaceful demonstrators. Yet despite
the severe economic and physical threats, Greenwood-based activists
persevered and the local movement continued to grow. Some of the most
exciting moments in Mississippi Civil Rights Movement history happened in Greenwood, especially when the black community held their
electric mass meetings, gatherings that activist Bob Moses once called
"an energy machine."[79] Amidst this level of organization and activity, the
Greenwood Freedom Schools opened their doors on July 6, 1964, just ten
days prior to this issue of The Freedom Carrier.*

Freedom Day in Greenwood!

Today all people who believe in freedom should join us for Freedom Day. Time and Time again we have tried to register for voting and Martha Lamb, the registrar for Leflore County, has turned Negroes away or has failed them. But we shall not let Martha discourage us. The more people she turns away, the more people must go to the courthouse.

Today marks the fourth Freedom Day in Greenwood. During the first Freedom Day, the courthouse was picketed, but no arrests were made. However, the second Freedom Day a large number of people were arrested. The last Freedom Day was without incident. We do not know what the outcome of today's Freedom Day will be, but whatever the outcome we will not let it stop us.

Many Negroes have been to the courthouse over and over only to be turned away by the white power that stands behind the counter. It is time to show the white people in Mississippi and people all over the United States that WE WANT TO VOTE AND THAT WE WILL NOT STOP TRYING UNTIL WE GET THE VOTE!! Today there will also be freedom registrars down at the courthouse so that anyone who wants to join the Freedom Democratic Party in Mississippi may do so.

Summer Violence

During a state's rights rally in Atlanta, Georgia three Freedom Singers were beaten unmercifully by a crowd. Chuck Neblett, Wilson Brown, and Matthew Jones arrived at the rally at 12:30 and by 1:00 they were being beaten with metal tables and chairs. Karen Haberman, a SNCC volunteer accompanied the three to the fair grounds but escaped without injury. The Freedom Singers were sent to the hospital with holes in their heads. The Negro keeper of the fair grounds was also injured.

In Greenwood, SNCC worker Phil Moore was beaten while canvassing in Baptist Town. Also, within the last week, two cars have turned up with slashed tires. One incident occurred while volunteers were inside the police station talking with the FBI about Phil Moore's assailant.

Church Ablaze—Firemen Gaze . . .

A Negro church in Browning, about three miles east of Greenwood, was burned to the ground early Saturday morning. As the Greenwood Fire Dept. arrived on the scene, the Pleasant Plain Missionary Baptist Church was spokesmen here believed that the burning had racial overtones. FBI agents went to the scene later on a COFO complaint. COFO said that the fire department did not attempt to extinguish the blaze. An assistant police chief, said that there was no source of water close to the church and that the water available on the truck was kept to protect buildings in the area.

Freedom School Opens

It is felt that the state of Mississippi has the worst educational system in the entire United States. As degraded as the white education is, the Negro has the worst half of the worst. A need to try to fill that gap was felt. Therefore COFO initiated the idea of Freedom Schools as an attempt to supplement the present system of education.

The first Freedom School to be established was open on July 6. The school will operate on a six weeks basis with a break after the first three weeks. Emphasis is being placed on Negro History and citizenship. English, Sciences, foreign languages, and creative writing are also being offered, as special subjects. Students are able to take two special subjects, in the afternoon, typing, art, drama, and journalism are offered to those interested. The Freedom Carrier is put out by the students in the journalism class. The students are responsible for the makeup of the entire paper.

Students are also being taught how to lay out leaflets and how to run the office machinery. Students also participate in folk singing workshops and work with voter registration in the distribution of leaflets throughout the community. For more information on the Freedom Schools you may call the office.

Register today!

Greenwood Grumbles Speaking of Freedom—
By Editor C. T.

We feel free when we can do as we please. We do not like it if anyone tries to stop us. Even a tiny baby will fly into rage if his hands are held so that he cannot move them. This is not exactly the love of freedom, for the baby has nothing in particular that he wants to do with his hands. It is more nearly hatred of restraint. But psychologists tell us that it is one of the few qualities found in all children from birth, and it is likely the basis for man's love of freedom.

Animals too often seem to want more freedom than they have. The dog strains at the leash to run free. The pet bird flies out of its cage when given the opportunity. Wild animals in zoos pace their cages hour by hour, ready to escape at the first chance. These animals are probably better cared for and fed than they would be if they were free. But animals, like men, crave the freedom to do as they choose.

The Negroes in Mississippi are fed up with the life here. We feel that it is time something was done to stop the killings or murders, the prejudice, the mistreatment of Negroes here. Freedom is a very precious thing to any race of people, but in a nation that is supposed to be free and where oppression still exists, something really has to be done. As our forefathers fought for this nation to be free, we also say to our oppressors "Give us freedom, or give us death."

Midway
By Naomi Long Madgett

I've come this far to
Freedom
And I won't turn back.
I'm changing to the

Highway
From my ole dirt track.
And I'm stretching and
I'm growing
And I'll reap what I've
Been sowing
Or my skin's not black,
I've prayed and slaved
And waited
And I've sung my song.
You've slashed me and
You've treed me
And you've everything
But freed me,
But in time you'll
You need me.
And it won't be long.
I've seen daylight
Breaking high above the
Bough.
I've found my destination
And I've made my vow:
So whether you abhor me
Or deride me or ignore
Me,
Mighty mountains loom
Before me,
And I won't stop now.

The Wind
By C. S.

The wind is a very
Strange thing.
The winter it will
Always bring.
Sometimes it brings

A full breeze.
That sends away the
Dried leaves.
It twirls and it
Whirls and
Leaves around,
Then all at once
It settles them down.

Note: C. S. is a student in the Freedom School. She will enter the eighth grade in the fall.

Our Thoughts

Q. Has the Civil Rights Movement been effective in Greenwood?

A. Yes, I think so, because more whites than I ever noticed before are becoming friendlier. There are some who are hostile, but only a few.—M. A.

A. No. Many whites still have their bitterness toward the Negro.—K. N.

A. Yes, I see many whites acting as though we are same race. Many persons of the white race have spoken and smiled at me.—Mrs. S. H.

A. No. White people have become more hostile toward the Negro since the movement came. They say they don't want any trouble, but since the Civil Rights Bill they say that that is <u>all</u> they have.—A. W.

Q. What is your reaction to Goldwater's nomination for President?

A. I don't like Goldwater. I don't think he should be President. He voted against the Civil Rights Bill, against the Peace Corps—against everything. I don't like the way he voted.—W. W.

A. I don't think he should be President. I figure if he ever win the Presidency I throw up my hands and holler "What's the use?" The way he voted against the Civil Rights Bill makes me think he's a southerner and a segregationist.—W. R.

FREEDOM NOW!

Hattiesburg Freedom Press

The Hattiesburg Freedom Press was produced by students in the Mt. Zion Freedom School of Hattiesburg, Mississippi. Mt. Zion was one of five Freedom Schools that met in Hattiesburg, the town that Freedom School coordinator Staughton Lynd dubbed "the Mecca of the Freedom School world." Hattiesburg was home to a vibrant black business community and was one of the first places SNCC gained a major foothold in Mississippi. Local people such as Victoria Jackson Gray, Peggy Jean Connor, Vernon Dahmer, J. C. Fairley, Daisy Harris Wade, and scores of others helped SNCC organize potential black voters in their community. By the summer of 1964, hundreds of African Americans had joined the local freedom movement, paving the way for the eventual success of the Hattiesburg Freedom Schools.

Throughout the 1960s, Mt. Zion became well known as a site for numerous civil rights meetings. Activity in the church only increased after Freedom Summer. Locals met there to discuss and plan boycotts, political strategies, and marches. Mt. Zion was also one of the last places Dr. Martin Luther King Jr. spoke before his death in the spring of 1968. Although the church has since been torn down and replaced by a new structure, its congregation remains proud of its historic role in the Civil Rights Movement. A historical marker now stands outside the new Mt. Zion Baptist Church celebrating its contributions to the black freedom struggle. The exact date of this issue of the Freedom Press is unknown, but several of the articles indicate that it was published during the final week of Freedom School classes. Perhaps the most interesting aspect of these essays are the testimonies written by Freedom School students who were going door-to-door in their community canvassing potential voters.

Our Day of Canvassing

On August 6, Linda B., Victoria J., my sister Gwendolyn and I went canvassing. It was a great experience because we had never been canvassing before.

We went to many houses. We are going to tell you about some very interesting things that happened.

We went to a house on Ruby Street and this is what we said to the lady there:

"Good evening. We are canvassing for the Mt. Zion Freedom School and we would like to know if you have ever been to Freedom School."

She said, "No! And I'm not going to Freedom School."

We asked her why and she said her "religion said she cannot go. And anyway, you little children don't know what you are doing. You don't know what freedom is."

"Oh yes we do," we said. "We know more than you know."

The lady kept on saying that we didn't know what we were talking about.

Another event was on Dumas Street. We went to a house of a mother who used to send her little girl to the Freedom School. But she had stopped letting her go. We asked the mother why.

She said, "Why, honey, she doesn't know anything about freedom. Besides, she has to keep the children because I have to go to work.

We had many other interesting times. These are just a few of them.

—Stephanie B.

The Town Nobody Loved
Lilly

I am writing a story about a town nobody loved or liked but did nothing about. I've been living here for fifteen years so I can tell you the story.

I was a little girl in the second grade when a terrible thing happened. There was a boy about 10 years of age and he was walking home from the store. I was walking home too, but I wasn't walking just beside him.

A little white girl came along riding her bicycle and the little colored boy stopped to look at her. The white girl stopped and said, "If you don't stop looking at me, nigger, I am going to tell my daddy that you were fighting with me."

The colored boy did not know that a colored boy was not supposed to look at a white girl and so he said, "I can look at you as long as I like."

The same night about ten o'clock a group of white men surrounded the boy's home and started shouting and saying, "Nigger, come on out. Don't make us come in and get you."

They went into the boy's home and took him out. He was hung the same night on Gulliver Hill.

But before anyone did anything about it the girl's family began getting letters saying their child was next.

How would this make the little boy live again? This isn't the answer to the Negro problem today but we must not let things like this happen again. Let's start to work now. Let's not stop till everyone is free.

Dear Gov. Johnson,

How are you? My name is Lynette. I am eleven years old and I am a Negro. I am going to the Mt. Zion Freedom School.

If you want to know why I am going there here are the reasons: I want to learn about my race; I want to become a part of history, I want to have the opportunity to learn here what I cannot learn in my regular school. I want to be able to vote when I am twenty-one. And I want to be a first-class citizen.

—Lynette Y.

A Friend Drops In

One of America's most famous folksingers is Peter Seeger. Last week he came to Mt. Zion to put on a special show for us.

Pete sang many songs about freedom. He said that in Africa the people have a special word for freedom. It is "lelapo."

Some of the songs that he sung for us were "Goodnight, Irene," "Oh Freedom," "What Did You Learn In School Today," and "Oh Healing River." He also sang a song about a giant that everybody liked, especially me.

Dick Kelley said he would have to pay three or four dollars in his city if he went to see Pete Seeger. He enjoyed the show. Calvin S. and John L. said they liked it also. Everett M. said that Pete Seeger was the best white man he ever heard sing like that.

At the end we sang "We Shall Overcome" and some of us cried.

—Anthony & Ratio

When the Wall Falls

On July 17th, I was out canvassing with Denis Jackson, one of the teachers at Mt. Zion Freedom School. We were trying to get the people to fill out Freedom Registration forms because there was going to be a convention the following day. The people gave us a hard time but we convinced some of them to fill out the forms. The people that wouldn't fill out the forms said they didn't want to have anything to do with it. One lady said she didn't believe anything was going to change in Mississippi. A lot of people said the same thing.

Then there are the people who won't fill out forms because they are afraid of losing their jobs. But what's holding back the people who don't have to work? Why aren't the people who are retired registering? Are they afraid? If so, of what or whom? Are they afraid of their freedom? Or the responsibilities they must assume in trying to obtain their freedom?

One lady said, "Why don't you let God take care of all this? He can do anything." I said, "You aren't the only person who thinks so. But what are we supposed to do? Sit around all the time and wait for God to do everything when we can do some things for ourselves?"

When I said that it really got her. But I didn't stop there. I was determined to get her to fill out an F. R. form. So I continued to talk to her about things like

The pride to feel that your own strength has cleared for you the way to heights to which you were not born, but struggled day by day.

The man who simply sits an' waits. For good to come along, ain't worth the breath that one would take to tell him he is wrong.

For good ain't flowin' 'round the world, for every fool to sup; You've got to put your see-ers on, and go an' hunt it up.

I quoted this from Paul L. Dunbar and while I was saying all of this to her I meant for it to hit and hit her hard.

I saw that she was responding to my conversation so I didn't stop there. I was determined. I wanted that lady's eyes opened wide so that she could see all the troublesome problems confronting the Negro people in Mississippi. I wanted her eyes opened wide so that she could see the things she could do.

I rendured another selection by a Negro poet named Melvin Tolsen. It goes like this

They tell us to forget Democracy is spurned, they tell us to forget the Bill of Rights is burned. Three hundred years we slaved We slave and suffer yet, though flesh and bone revel, they tell us to forget!

Oh, how can we forget our human rights denied? Oh how can we forget our manhood crucified? When justice is profaned and plea with curse is met, when freedom's gate is barred, oh, how can we forget?

It did the trick. I felt so glad and happy because I had opened up another world. I had torn down the wall.

What Freedom Means

Freedom to me means I can where I wnat to.

I can go to the white's picture shows and the café.

I want to go to a bathroom without seeing a sign that says "White Only" and "Negro Only."

I would like to go to a store and be served without being asked to get out.

That's what freedom means to me.

—Benton D.

A Visitor Comes to Town

George Ballis came to Hattiesburg to take pictures of the Freedom Schools. He is a photographer for the Southern Documentary Project. He has been a photographer for twelve years.

George has been to Philadelphia, Greenwood, Meridain, Ruleville and Jackson besides coming here to Hattiesburg.

George was here in Hattiesburg last January when they had the march on the courthouse. He has found that the police don't bother the people as much today as they did in January.

—Cynthia P.

Freedom Quiz

Who Am I??????

1.) The Civil War was over and slowly the Southern states returned to the Union. There were many new faces that were new in the Congress from the Southern states. One of the faces that was new came from Mississippi. It was the face of the first Negro Congressman ever elected. His name was????????
2.) I am the lawyer who went before the most important court in America to protest segregation in the schools in 1954. My name is?????

What the Summer Has Meant To Me

I think the summer has made a lot of changes in Mississippi. Now we can sit down and eat at Woolworth's and Kress'.

I think the summer has made the white men see that we are not happy with Mississippi. We want to make even more changes.

I think that next summer we can get to go to more than just two places in Hattiesburg. We should be able to go to the drive-in.

—Mattie M.

The Meaning of Freedom

Freedom Means:

1.) Waking up each morning and be glad you were born.
2.) Playing "Doctor, Lawyer, Indian Chief" and mean it.
3.) Not trying to wash away the color of your skin with soap.
4.) Not changing your last name so people won't know what your religion is.
5.) "Mr." and "Mrs."
6.) "Bad" hair is really "good."
7.) Reading the Declaration of Independence for the first time.

—Douglas Tuchman [Freedom School teacher]

One Person's Prayer.

DEAR GOD, THE FATHER OF MANKIND, MADE ME THE WAY I AM. HE DIDN'T MAKE ME YELLOW LIKE JUDY, HE DIDN'T MAKE ME WHITE LIKE SAM.

WHEN GOD CREATED YOU AND ME HE DIDN'T FAVOR ONE COLOR, YOU SEE YET IN THIS GREAT BIG WORLD OF STRIFE, THE RACES TAKE EACH OTHER'S LIVES.

THEY HATE US NOT FOR WHAT WE ARE, BUT BECAUSE OF THE COLOR OF OUR SKIN, YET DEEP DOWN IN THEIR HEARTS THEY KNOW THAT OUR CREATOR MADE US KIN.

I AM A NEGRO, YOU SEE, I KNOW THAT GOD CREATED ME MY PARENTS WERE ALSO EVE AND ADAM, SO I DON'T THINK I'M INFERIOR, MADAM.

WE ARE THE PARENTS OF THE WORLD OF EVERY BOY AND GIRL BORN SO WE SHOULD LEARN TO LOVE ONE ANOTHER AS IF CHILD WERE OUR OWN.

* MRS. JIMMIE C.

The Story of Rev. Klunder.

Rev. Bruce Klunder was a hero for freedom. He believed that freedom could only be won if people worked for it every minute of the day.

One day in Cleveland he lay down behind a bulldozer to stop the building of a segregated school. The driver of the bulldozer didn't see Rev. Klunder when he backed up the machine. Rev. Klunder was killed immediately.

If we want to have our freedom we must remember what other people have sacrificed and try harder ourselves.

—Anthony H.

The Great Debate

Last Sunday was a big day for many of the freedom school students. A big debate took place at St. Paul's Church between teams from Mt. Zion, Moss Point, Morningstar, and Priest's Creek. The big question was "Which is the best way to gain equality" violence or non-violence? Each school picked the side it thought was the right one. Mt. Zion won two debates. It was fun.

Looking Back

What has the summer accomplished? I think it has started more colored people registering to vote than had tried before. It was also an experience because white people came to live with Negroes. Kress' and Woolworth's also opened up their lunch counters.

I thought that when COFO came to set up its project it would lead to trouble, even though it wasn't their purpose. Maybe the reason why there wasn't any trouble was because the people who didn't like COFO thought it wasn't doing enough to get them aroused.

I would like people to live in unity. People should get to know each other. They should become better educated to show that one person is as good as another. We should also have equal facilities for everybody.

—Willie M.

Student Voice of True Light (Hattiesburg, MS)

The Student Voice of True Light was produced by the Freedom School students attending classes at the True Light Baptist Church located in the heart of Hattiesburg's historic black community the Mobile Street District. Originally organized in 1903, True Light Baptist had for years been a center of local African American community organizing. Black women formed the core of this tradition. For more than six decades, they had helped raise money, provide meals, pay bills, and organize numerous social aid societies to assist local black families in need. Furthermore, the Student Voice of True Light was not the first African American newspaper produced by True Light church members. Over thirty years before Freedom Summer, True Light's congregation joined with several other local black churches to produce a black community newspaper. This long legacy of community organizing established an institutional tradition of activism that helped make True Light the site of one of Mississippi's largest and most active Freedom Schools. Its student body required a large faculty that ranged between eight and ten teachers depending on space and demand. As is clear in the essays that follow, many of True Light's Freedom School students were particularly interested in critiquing their discriminatory society and thinking of ways to redefine freedom.

July 20, 1964

What I Don't Like about Hattiesburg

There are lots of things I don't like about Hattiesburg. One thing is the bus drivers, which have already been brought to light to the eyes of the people. Bus drivers, as Shirley White describes, are terrible. I have never had any of the incidents happen to me because when I was young I learned we were supposed to sit in the back part of the bus. I'm not going to sit in the back anymore.

The one thing I don't like is these Jim Crow restaurants. What I mean by that is these places where they allow no one but white

Front cover of the Hattiesburg *Student Voice of True Light*.
Courtesy of the McCain Library and Archives, University of Southern Mississippi.

skinned people to eat and not people with black skins. Since the bill passed I eat where I want to.

The question that puzzles me is: Why couldn't we eat in these places before the Civil Rights Bill was passed? I know because we have black skin, but what has that to do with it. The black skinned people have fought in the war, become great scientists, and are qualified for the same jobs. All together we belong to America as much as the whites do. We were all created equal. Neither race is superior to the other.

—Larry B., age 13

When I Was Going on Hardy Street

Well, it was this bus driver. I was on the first straight seat on the bus, and he told me to move back. I said, "I will not. I paid a dime and two pennies for a transfer and I'm not moving." He said, "You know white people must get on this bus." I said, "You know colored people must get on this bus too."

—Mattie Jean Wilson, age 10

Editor: Mattie Jan Wilson
Assistant Editor—Shirley White
Managing Editor—Jimmie R. Ratliff
Circulation Manager—Janice Walton
Reporter—Albert J. Evans

Mississippi Freedom Democratic Party precinct meeting, Saturday, July 25, St. Paul's Methodist Church on 5th Street at four o'clock.

There will be a meeting for everyone interested in working on the Student Voice of True Light on Monday, July 20, at 2:30 in the afternoon, at the True Light Baptist Church. A new staff for this week's issue will be elected at this meeting.

Why I Deserve Freedom

I am a Negro, I am a black man. And, because of my color, I am deprived of the human rights which are given to me by God and promised to me by the United States. I live in a country of free people, yet I am not free.

Our great nation was conceived in liberty and dedicated to the proposition that all men are created equal.

The Bill of Rights guarantees to everyone the freedoms of religion, and the right of peaceful assembly, but in Mississippi these rights are denied to Negroes. The 13th Amendment abolished slavery. I deserve freedom because the law of the land states this.

The Negroes of the past have fought for freedom inside and outside the United States. Crispus Attucks, a man of Negro blood, was the first to be killed in the struggle to free our great nation from its mother country. He was described by Poet John Boyle O'Reilly as "the first to defy and the first to die." Thus, history has recorded that I have a stake in freedom.

If necessary, I will die in order to have freedom for my people.

Today I am the world's footstool but tomorrow I hope to be one of its leaders. By attending freedom school this summer I am preparing for that tomorrow.

—Albert J. Evans, age 15

A Look at Negro Hospitals and Doctors

Have you ever thought about why the Negro doctors do not perform any operations and take X-Rays of their own patients in the hospital?

I have always wanted to become a doctor. I would like to study in a medical school that is not segregated.

—Spencer W., age 14

An Interview with Bessie Jean H.

1. Have you tried to eat in a restaurant since the Civil Rights Bill has been passed? "Yes!"
2. Where? "Woolworth's and Kress's."
3. Did they serve you? "Yes."
4. Did some of the people leave? "Yes."
5. Are you going again? "Oh, yes."

—Susie A., age 14

This I Have Learned in Freedom School

I have learned most of all that the Negro is really just as superior as another race. If the Negro has a good education, he can make as big a success as any man from another race.

I also learned that a Negro was the first to give up his life for American freedom, and from then on the Negro has been giving up his life for the American cause.

The Negro isn't really free until he knows and acts like he's free. Just because the Civil Rights Bill has been passed doesn't mean he's free.

Freedom for the Negroes isn't just the right to eat where another race eats or go where another race goes but to be able to learn the same things that another race learns and be able to express themselves the way they want without being afraid of what might happen to them.

—Sandra Jo-Ann O., age 16

A Story of Mexico

Once there was a family who lived in Mexico. They stayed in the valley. There was a volcano over the hill which the family did not know was there.

The volcano exploded. All the people saw the great fires of the volcano. Then the people started to run. The volcano cooled down.

The family was found dead in their house. A girl and a boy and the mother and father were found.

—Sandra K., age 11

What I Think About Hattiesburg

Hattiesburg is an unfit place to live because of the people that make up this town. The whites have their way. If they kill one of us they get away with it, but if we kill one of them they kill us. What are we going to do about this? Nothing but take our stand for our equal rights.

—Shirley White, age 14

An Interview

July 15 I interviewed a student. This student has been to both Woolworth's and Kress's. She says, "I wasn't really hungry, but I went because I wanted to prove to the whites that I could eat in public places just as they could." While she was eating a small group of whites walked out. A crowd of people was watching her.

—Janice Walton, age 14

Freedom

There's a bell in Philadelphia with a crack in it. Written on it is the legend: "Proclaim liberty throughout the land, and to all the inhabitants thereof."

We are now observing the ultimate expression of the simple idea that freedom is the natural right of all men, no matter what their race, creed, or place of birth is.

It is well to remember that even now, about 100 years after Abe Lincoln signed the Proclamation, the world has been half slave (Negroes) and half free (Whites). Only now there are people suffering slavery of the spirit, instead of physical bondage. Their masters seek to enslave their minds, too. They say they are selling equality, but there is no freedom.

All men are equal, but they are not the same. There are friendly men, greedy men, kind men, generous men, mean men, cowardly men, clever men, stubborn men, and honest men. They come in all sizes, shapes, and only one difference, the color of their skin.

—submitted by Jimmie R. Ratliff, age 14

Slavery

Slavery hindered us from making any progress. Webster defines it as being in entire subjugation to the will of another. Slavery enslaves one's mind as well as the condition in which he lives. I believe if it hadn't been for slavery, our race would not be in the shape it is in today. During slavery the white man enslaved the slave's mind, so as to keep him down below him. I think slavery was a terrible thing because it left all the slaves ignorant and untrained. The slave took orders from the master; he was not used to being his own boss.

During slavery there were many revolts. One of these revolts was known as the Nat Turner Revolt. It involved a Negro by the name of Nat Turner who had a vision from God, telling him to kill the white people and make them the last, instead of the first. He carried out this vision, and after two months' time was hanged. This is just an example of many slave revolts.

I believe there are many people still in slavery today. They are enslaved by the white race. They feel that they must still look up to the white race as their superiors. As I close my essay on slavery, I think that it hinders the Negro from making any progress.

I hope that in the future we as Negroes will strive harder for our coming tomorrow.

—Beverly H., age 14

An Interview with Miss Patterson

Miss Patterson, 26, is from New York City:

1. What do you think of Hattiesburg? "I think there is a lot of work to be done here."
2. Were you at the world's fair? "Yes, I was a picket."
3. Have you ever been arrested? "Yes, at the world's fair."
4. What do you think of the Freedom School? "I enjoy myself very much. I meet a lot of wonderful people."
5. Have you had any troubles with the people of Hattiesburg? "No, I haven't."

—Odis Ruth T., age 11

My Brother on a Bus

My brother was coming from 25th Avenue off Hardy Street. This was a young bus driver and he told my brother to get up. My brother said, "You make me get up." The driver pressed hard on the brakes and said, "Take this dime and get off my bus." My brother started to the back but then he thought of what my other brother said and went to the front door. The driver acted like he would not open the front door, so my brother sat down. So the driver opened the front door and my brother got off and walked.

—Mattie Jean Wilson, age 10

Two Letters

Dear Pre ident Johnson,

We are in the 8th and 9th grade class of Freedom School in the state of Mississippi. We are measuring the distance around the tops of our freedom schools. We use our own spirit as the unit of measurement. Since the President is the most important person in our country, we decided we would use your spirit so as to make us free from slavery. We will call it a "Johnson" and measure our freedom school in "Johnsons."

We know you are a busy man, but could you send us your own freedom measurement?

Yours truly,
Shelley S., age 13

Dear President Johnson,

There are many holidays on the calendar. There is a Mother's Day, there is a Father's Day, and there is a Ground Hog Day. But why isn't there a Freedom Day for Negroes?

Yours truly,
Shelley S., age 13

◆   ◆   ◆

July 24, 1964

Mississippi Freedom Democratic Party

The Mississippi Freedom Democratic Party was organized in Mississippi to let the people in Mississippi know that the regular Democratic Party does not represent all the people of Mississippi. The black people of Mississippi have challenged the regular

Democratic party and are going to take matters into their own hands.

At the Democratic Convention in August we will challenge the seating of the regular Democratic Party. We are going to let the people know in the Northern states as well as in the Southern states that we are not satisfied with the Democratic Party here, because we are not represented here in Mississippi as citizens.

We also want the people to know that there are Negroes in the South who really want to vote but are not allowed the right to vote.

We have Negroes here who are going to attend the Precinct Meetings, the County, the District and the State meetings, and the National Democratic Convention.

These are our reasons for organizing the Mississippi Freedom Democratic Party.

—Sandra Elaine D., age 16

What We Want

Resolutions for the Precinct Meetings, prepared by 5,6, and 7 year-olds at True Light Freedom School.
1. Freedom
2. Parks for black and white
3. Better roads and streets
4. Swimming pool near True Light
5. A new mayor

The Will to be Free

History tells us that men have lived and died in slavery. But it has been an unwanted slavery. The desire to be free was born with man. It has lived always. Freedom has not always been the law of the land, but it has always been the law of the heart.

The struggle for freedom is an old, old story. It began with the first man before the days of written history. It is still going on today. The people of yesterday were much the same as the people of today. They had the same feelings, the same desires, and the same ambitions. The people of the United States believe they have the right to "life, liberty, and the pursuit of happiness." In the long struggle for freedom, have other men also believed in these same ideals and privileges?

Suggested for inclusion by Glenda B., age 15, 9th grade

Attend the Library Precinct Meeting—Mississippi Freedom Democratic Party
July 25, 4:00 PM, St. Paul's Church.

An Interview with Mrs. M. L. V.

How long did you know Mr. Clyde Kennard? Most all of my life. I went to school with him.

Was he a Sunday School teacher? Yes, at Mary Magdalene Baptist Church.

Did you know when he was framed about the whiskey? Yes, I was working on the college campus at the time of his arrest, but I didn't see his arrest in person. I was working for a man who was from up North. The man came in for dinner and he asked me if I had heard the news over the radio. I said, "No, why, what happened?" He said they arrested Kennard. I asked what for. He said someone planted some whiskey in his car while he was trying to enroll. He said when he came out of the building the police were waiting for him. They didn't have any other way to bother him so they arrested him for transporting whiskey. That's the one way they had to keep him from enrolling he said. He said he couldn't say too much concerning this! He got out of that. Next thing they got an Uncle Tom to frame him some other way. They paid him because he worked at farmers feed. This Uncle Tom stole some feed in the daytime. At around 3:00 he got the feed and carried it to Kennard's house and tried to sell the feed to Kennard. After that they took it and the police went and got the feed and arrested him the second time.

How long did he stay in jail? He stayed in jail so long he began to get sick.

When he went to prison what happened? Different organizations took up money to get him a doctor or some medicine, but they wouldn't let him have medical care.

Did they feed him the proper food? No, they didn't feed him the proper food to eat so he went to work on an empty stomach. A man offered to do his work when he got sick, but they wouldn't let him do it.

Did he come from a good family? Yes, he did. They were quiet and Christian-like and very friendly toward people.

—Shirley White, age 14, 9th grade

America Today

America is a great land of great people; it is said to be a free land of free people, and a modern land of people with modern ideas. Some of these ideas are small, some are large, some are right, and some are wrong.

My idea of freedom in America is that it is a land half slave— the Negroes—and half free—whites. America has come a long way in the struggle for freedom, yet it has a long way to go. No one can be completely free, for there are laws of nature and man. But after all, everyone in America does not enjoy the freedom it offers.

—Albert J. Evans, age 15

What I Think About Mississippi

I think Mississippi is an unfit place to live because of the Southern White people.

The Southern white people do not want to see the Negro succeed, or any other race with black skin and kinky hair. The white people in the South and many other places have always classed the Negro lower than a dog.

Mississippi is a place where Negroes are not allowed to stand on their own feet.

We shall not be moved. The Southern whites and Jim Crows are not going to run us out of Mississippi.

—Terry M., age 10

What I Think About Hattiesburg

I think this is the hardest place to try to live in. I have several reasons for saying this. The white people are saying, let white be white. If they should go in places where Negroes are eating, they advise other white people to pay for whatever they ordered and walk out and leave it! I think the Negroes should take a stand. If you are working in a place and they refuse to serve Negroes, the colored workers there should walk out and let whites do the work.

Now we have integrated Kress's and Woolworth's. We should move on a little further. We should go in other places because the whites are being hard on Kress's and Woolworth's. We should go on to drug stores and other places. If they refuse to serve us, we should sit a little while, then walk out before they call the police for disturbing the peace. After we leave we should go back another day and try again.

—Mrs. Mable L. V.

What is Freedom?

Freedom is a very needed and important thing in our lives. I think if there were no freedom the world would be lost. When you are free, you can be somebody. When you are locked in and not free you don't have a chance to express yourself, not prove yourself to yourself. When you are not free you are afraid. When you are free, you are not afraid in a sense. When you are free you can love your fellow man whether he be black or white. When you are not free you have mostly hate in your heart for your fellow man. Pray that God will bless America and bless the greedy white people.

—Anna Lee S., 9th grade, age 13

Freedom

Freedom is like a note, that rings out loud.
Freedom is like gold, pounds for pounds.
Freedom is a road that never ends, that has no who, where, or
when.
Freedom is like a poem that rhymes, that means freedom for his
people,
her people, yours and mine.

—Rena Mae C., age 13

Freedom and What it Means to Me

Freedom is more than a big bunch of words. It has a meaning behind it. Freedom meant so much to Frederick Douglass that he was beaten for it. He believed that every Negro should be free. He taught Sunday School on the plantation and those slave owners told him he better quit or else they were going to shoot him. When Frederick Douglass was on his slave owner's plantation he was beaten with whips and sticks and kicked like a dog. He was found in a ditch bleeding and near death. The owner poured salt on the Negro's wounds. And Nathan Hale said, "Give me liberty or give me death."

Robert E. Lee had 1,000 slaves and he would rather have died than give them up. The same thing is true in the South today. The segregationists would rather die than give in to the Negroes. They are still killing Negroes.

—John Wesley D., 9th grade, age 17

An Interview with Mr. William D. Jones

Mr. Jones's home is on Long Island, New York. He was born in Birmingham, Alabama and has been living on Long Island for two years. His reason for coming here is that he is committed to the fight for freedom and since there is much less of it in Mississippi than in any other state, he was "drafted by my conscience, irrespective of the grave danger."

He thinks Hattiesburg is one of the worst places he has been in in the U.S., even though it is much better than most cities in Mississippi.

He was in Mississippi before, during World War II, and, coincidentally, he was discharged from the Army at Camp Shelby near Hattiesburg. "On my way home to Birmingham I went into a drugstore near the bus station in order to buy some film. I was kept waiting while white people who came after I did were waited on ahead of me. I demanded service, and the proprietor told me that just because I had on the uniform it did not make me any better than any other nigger. I walked out angrily and told him that I would return to Hattiesburg one of these days, and, like General MacArthur, I have returned. Just by a miracle I was assigned to Hattiesburg by COFO."

Mr. Jones has been arrested for civil rights activities. In fact, he is out on bail now for demonstrating at the opening of the New York World's Fair on April 22. His trial will be in New York on August 25.

Mr. Jones has been teaching for six years in public schools. He taught high school French and English in Alabama and Georgia.

He now teaches French in an all white elementary school where he has been for two years. Though he makes a more than average salary, he says, "I would accept a teaching position anywhere in Mississippi if I could get one, regardless of the meager salary, because I want to be a little closer to the real problems of my people and help as much as I can. I hope that my summer work in Mississippi will be of some lasting good to the young people of Hattiesburg."

—France D., age 14

There's just one Negro in the picture and he's a waiter. In other words, it seems that the Negroes only ride trains as waiters for the whites. The white man is still ordering the Negro around, and it's showing that in the dining cars and other sections of the train there still might be some segregation. It shows graphically that the white man trusts a Negro to bring his food to him, to wait on him and cook for him, yet he doesn't want the Negro to eat or sit with him.

This picture is not so typical today since Negroes have the right to ride in any coach and eat in the diners, and most of them do.

The problem is to get television, newspapers, movies, and advertisements to show Negro people as ordinary people in American life.

—Sandra Jo-Ann O., age 16

Freedom

Freedom is a seven letter word with a great meaning. To many people, and myself, it is one of the greatest words when we are actually free. What I mean by free is to go to any place you want to without being involved in violence and being able to speak as you please.

Why don't white people want us to eat in the same places they eat? We are all human beings and God made us all. We can't help what color our skin is! When you are free it doesn't just mean to eat where you want to but to be free where it counts most and that is in your own mind. Then you can really tell yourself you are free and really mean it.

—Larry B., 8th grade, age 13

* *

Editor: Shirley White
Art Work: Alan Johnson

One class saw the advertisement above, which shows people on a Vista-Dome train. Everyone in the picture is white, except the waiter who is serving them. A caption under the picture says, "People like you, people you like—ride the train." Several students in the class wrote of their impressions of this picture.

While looking at the picture a thought came to my mind. Here in the picture is a group of white passengers on a train and one Negro, but he just happens to be a waiter. Everyone seems to be enjoying himself very much, but I wonder about the waiter.

—Otis M.

◆　　◆　　◆

Undated Issue

I don't like the angry people up town because they are so mean. The man that drives the bus took the girl's money instead of her transfer. He wouldn't give it back. He said once it gets into that little thing you can't get it out. And she was mad at him from then on.

—Bessie Ann D.

What I Think about Hattiesburg

I think it is a no good place and it could be a better city. I hope that Goldwater won't be our president because he hates Negroes and we need one that loves both black and white. I think that we are free to eat anywhere we wish and stand for our equal rights. I am glad that the Civil Rights Bill was passed because whites can go to any show. And we could go to any show they go to.

—Odis Ruth T.
Brenda Lynn E.

Freedom school is nice. We learned all sorts of things. We learned that Crispus Attucks was the first man to die for America's freedom. We learned that Negroes have been in America for 345 years.

Why Are Negroes Treated Badly?

Negroes are treated badly because of the color of their skin. They are hit with guns, sticks, bricks, and bottles. I think as citizens of the United States we should have our own freedom of speech. I will be sad when they find those missing men dead. The song of the Negro's cry is we shall overcome. And I believe that we will overcome someday. It is a good thing that we are trying to fight for freedom. I am very little and my skin is black. But I think I am still a citizen of Hattiesburg.

—Willie A. C.

Thursday several reporters interviewed a student from Rowan Senior High School. Her replies follow:

A Look at Hattiesburg

Bus Drivers

A bus driver slapped a Negro woman because she didn't move farther back in the bus so a white woman could have a seat.

A Negro woman was sitting in front of the bus when the bus driver asked her to move back so a white man could have a seat, but instead of moving back the woman told the bus driver, "I've been sitting in the back a little too long and I should be sitting closer now to the front."

School

This Negro student doesn't think the schools are as well equipped as the white students' schools. An example she gave was about books. When Negro schools need new books they get their books from the white schools and the white schools get the new books.

—Janice W.

Some Opinions of Dennis F. C. and What He Is Going to Do

Dennis F. C. thinks Goldwater will win. But he is behind Scranton. He does plan to join the NAACP. After the 12th grade he is going to college and get his Master's degree and go on to the Marines. By the time he gets out of the Marines things will be better. For a living he is going to play football.

—Kenneth A.

One of Jackson's largest hotels, the Robert E. Lee Hotel, has closed to keep from admitting Negroes. I think we Negroes ought to be proud of color. Because God gave it to us.

—Robert T.

1. What do you think of Hattiesburg? "I think Hattiesburg needs to be developed so everyone could have his equal rights."
2. Were you born in Hattiesburg? "Oh yes!"
3. Have you ever tried to eat in a restaurant before the Civil Rights Bill was passed? "Yes I have, Woolworth's."
4. Did they serve you? "No, they didn't. They told me to go to the end of the counter, but I didn't. I walked out."
5. Have you tried to eat since the Civil Rights Bill has been passed? "No, but I am going soon."
6. Why didn't you go sooner? "I didn't have time."

—Larry B.

An Interview with Mrs. Nancy Ellin

Mrs. Nancy Ellin, 28, of Kalamazoo, Mich. gave her opinion on Hattiesburg and Kalamazoo.

Mrs. Ellin has been living in Kalamazoo, Mich. for 2 years. She has been married for 2 and a half years. She has no children. Mrs. Ellin doesn't like Kalamazoo because the people there are too satisfied.

Mrs. Ellin has seen one part of Hattiesburg. She thinks that the streets ought to have street lights and they ought to be paved. Mrs. Ellin thinks the freedom schools are a very good idea.

She plans to work with the N.A.A.C.P. when she returns to Kalamazoo.

—Audrey E.

My sister was going to Chicago on the bus and a white lady came and told her would you get up and let me sit down. My sister and I paid my money just like you and I'm going to sit right here.

—Bessie Ann D.

The Freedom School

The Freedom School, I think, is a great opportunity for everyone young and old. If you are in school it isn't any harm to attend Freedom School. If you are old, it will be a great help in registering to vote. I wish everyone that could would attend. In Freedom School you can learn a lot. You have the same subjects you take in school.

I think there is a lot we can do to help. We could go and ask people to attend Freedom School. They might have small children and you could offer to keep them while they attend some of the classes if they attend different classes than you do. It will be a great help to them. I am going to do all that I can to help. I hope that you will too.

—Sandra W.

This Is What Happens in Hattiesburg

During the month of April while marching on the picket line, a friend of mine, among others, was picked up. Lawrence G. was picked up for nothing.

A boy was trying to get on the bus in town and the bus driver said, "Hurry up," and a girl spoke up and said, "He's not going to get killed trying to get on the bus."

After the civil rights bill was passed, Negroes didn't want to go in restaurants, but two or three days later they began to go in the restaurant. Most of them are still afraid to go in these places because they are afraid they could be attacked.

—Shirley W.

Freedom

Freedom is a small word but it has great meanings. Webster says it is a state of being free and independent. There are many ways in which we can get our freedom. We may protest, or we may even try to integrate public places. I believe we cannot get our freedom (equal rights) by violent movements. Violence hinders progress and may cause severe destruction. I also believe we should fight with our intelligence instead of with our fists. We can win this war if we really press forward and try. I believe we could help matters a lot better if more of our people would attend the freedom schools. In the schools they would be taught subjects that are not taught in public schools. They would be taught how to register to vote, which every person 21 or over should be able to do. I think the freedom schools are helping our race a great deal, to set a goal for a better tomorrow.

—Beverly H.

We have overcome slavery. Negroes shall become better citizens. Negroes shall have better jobs. We will not struggle any more. We haven't got all our rights yet, but freedom is all we want.

—Edwin E. P.

Sometimes when Negro people catch the bus and take a seat in the front seat the bus driver says go to the back. But when some white people get on they sit anywhere they want. Sometimes the bus driver makes the colored people get off when they make a lot of noise. I don't have this problem because I don't ride the bus.

—Barbara Ann R.

The World's Fair

The World's Fair is a very exciting place to visit. I only went three times, but I enjoyed myself very much. The food was one point of interest—sampling food from different parts of the world. I enjoyed the General Electric Pavilion. It showed us how far we had come with the help of electricity and how far we will go in the years to come. The General Motors Pavilion took us back to prehistoric times—the time of the cave man, the discovery of the wheel, and the invention of fire.

I hope to go back to the Fair before it closes and see some more things, maybe next year. It would be a very nice place for everyone to go that could.

—Sandra W.

On November 22nd at 2:15 John F. Kennedy was shot and killed in Dallas, Texas. At the time of his death Mrs. Kennedy and the Vice President were with the President. The flags were down half mast during the President's burial. The whole nation was able to see the burial of the President.

—Gladys T.

What I Think of Texas

When I first went there I liked it very well. But after I came back and the President got shot, I didn't like it any more.

—Barbara L.

Happiness is. . . . . going to public places.
Happiness is. . . . . going to places without being looked at.

—Anita Louise H.

A Story

Once upon a time there was a lady. She lived at 1100 7th St. Her name was Miss Snowball. When I was a little girl she used to have church at her house. One morning we went down to her house for church and her husband was a preacher. He came so we each had a Bible verse to learn. So he said, "I saw something in the sky this morning." We asked him what he saw. He said, "I think it was a chicken." And so he went on talking. He said, "I saw something white last night when I was sleeping." We asked him, "What was it?" He said it was some ghost. He said it was a little five year old baby and it was a lady. She just kept buzzing in his ear and so that ran him crazy. So the old man died and they kept worrying his wife so she died. But these are the last words she said, "They kill me but I'm going to heaven or to hell."

—Gwen B.

Freedom Day

Freedom Day is everywhere
Freedom people here and there
Jump up and down—
Join the people from out of town—
To make this a happy Freedom Day.
I want to be free,
I know you do too—
So don't sit around
Start marching along for your
F-R-E-E-D-O-M

—Alma T.

"Dear _____" Letters

Dear President Johnson,

I hope that I am not hurting your feelings.

We want our freedom. So you better help us to get our freedom.

We do not want the policeman to beat up any one else. The Civil Rights Bill has passed. I tell you again we want freedom. I go to Freedom School.

Yours truly,
Donny E.

Dear President Johnson,

I'm asking you for our freedom. Will you give us our freedom? Do you know how we feel without our freedom and we are working hard to get it. I'm asking you to please give it to us.

Your friend,
Dennis B.

Dear President Johnson,

Thank you for signing the Civil Rights Bill. We are so glad to know that someone is on our side. But some of the white people are friendly down here. We all want our freedom. And we are going to get it some day if we have to die for it.

Yours truly,
Linda D.

Dear President Johnson,

I go to Freedom School. I have learned a few freedom songs. We are asking you to send more people down here to protect the people and Civil Rights workers in this state. Then there will be no more bombing and fighting.

Yours truly,
Anthony E.

Who Am I?

Who am I, let me see,
Am I a dog or am I a bee?
Am I a princess who's sweet and kind?
Am I a maniac who's out of her mind?
I think I know and I'll tell you
I'm not the girl I used to be.

Who am I? I have to know
So I may tell it wherever I go.

Student Voice of True Light (Hattiesburg, MS)

I'll tell it to men of all the land.
I'll tell it to kids who shake my hand,
That I am free and it shows
To everyone over all the land.

Who am I? I'll tell you now,
I'll have to find words, but I'll tell it somehow.
I am a Negro who fought her best
To earn her freedom and deserves to rest.
So do as I did, and you'll be free,
Just don't hit back, and you'll win
Your rest.

—Sandra Jo-Ann O.

A scene from Freedom School teacher orientation in Oxford, OH. Courtesy of Herbert Randall and the McCain Library and Archives, University of Southern Mississippi.

Young students in a Freedom School classroom. Courtesy of Herbert Randall and the McCain Library and Archives, University of Southern Mississippi.

Outdoor Freedom School class. Courtesy of Herbert Randall and the McCain Library and Archives, University of Southern Mississippi.

Hattiesburg Freedom School students meeting on the steps of the Mt. Zion Baptist Church. Courtesy of Herbert Randall and the McCain Library and Archives, University of Southern Mississippi.

Young Freedom School student working on a writing project. Courtesy of Herbert Randall and the McCain Library and Archives, University of Southern Mississippi.

A group of Freedom School students, trying to stay cool and distracted by outside activity. Courtes of Herbert Randall and the McCain Library and Archives, University of Southern Mississippi.

Freedom School teacher Arthur Reese from Detroit. Courtesy of Herbert Randall and the McCain Library and Archives, University of Southern Mississippi.

Freedom School guitar lesson. Courtesy of Herbert Randall and the McCain Library and Archives, University of Southern Mississippi.

Palmer's Crossing Freedom School student Larry Lee. Courtesy of Herbert Randall and the McCain Library and Archives, University of Southern Mississippi.

Young Girls at Freedom School. Courtesy of Herbert Randall and the McCain Library and Archives, University of Southern Mississippi.

Freedom School students and teachers at the Mississippi Freedom School Convention. Courtesy of the Wisconsin Historical Society.

Freedom School students singing at the Mississippi Freedom School Convention.
Courtesy of the Wisconsin Historical Society.

The Freedom News (Holly Springs, MS)

Published during the first full week of Freedom School classes, The Freedom News from Holly Springs was one of the first Freedom School newspapers produced during Freedom Summer. The vibrant Holly Springs Freedom School met in two small houses located just across the campus of Rust College, one of the nation's oldest historically black institutions of higher learning and the alma mater of black journalism pioneer Ida B. Wells. Some of the teachers were housed in the Rust dorms. When Holly Springs Freedom School classes ended at 4 p.m. on weekday afternoons, local organizers hosted adult literacy classes, allowing people of all ages to attend the Holly Springs Freedom School.

Reports out of Holly Springs indicated a powerful Freedom School experience for both students and teachers. One of the Holly Springs teachers wrote that "[t]he atmosphere in class is unbelievable. It is what every teacher dreams about—real, honest enthusiasm and the desire to learn anything and everything."[80] One of the regular students was a twenty-five-year-old wife and mother who often stayed after classes to practice writing extra essays, passionately striving to improve her literacy and grammar while making an immense impression on her teachers. Many of the younger Freedom School students were just as impressive and particularly inspired their teachers by writing and performing a play based on the life of Mississippi civil rights activist Medgar Evers.

July 8, 1964

The Three Who Are Missing

How do we as Negroes feel about the freedom workers coming into Mississippi is a question many are asking. After asking many of my friends and neighbors I have heard them say "It's a miracle" or "at least our prayers are being answered." To us this is one of the most wonderful things that has happened since we were actually freed from slavery. We know these people didn't

the freedom news

VOL. I NO.1   July 8, 1964

Published by the members of the Holly Springs Freedom School

THE THREE WHO ARE MISSING

How do we as Negroes feel about the freedom workers coming into Mississippi is a question many are asking. After asking many of my friends and neighbors I have heard them say "It's a miracle" or "at least our prayers are being answered." To us this is one of the most wonderful things that has happened since we were actually freed from slavery. We know these people didn't have to give up their precious time and come here to help us and we know that they are here because of love. Love not only for us, but also because they love the United States. They know that before the United States can have the respect of other countries it must also have the respect of its own people, both Negro and white.

When we heard about the three freedom workers missing, we were hurt, but not shocked because many of our people have come up missing and nothing was said or done about it. Ever since I can remember I have been told of such cases from my people, but never have I heard it said on the news or over the T.V. or radio. This was known only to a few of us, not nation-wide. X Even though most of us have given up hope about the three freedom workers, we are praying that they will be found alive.

The freedom workers have the blessings and prayers of the Negroes in Mississippi. We will be forever grateful.

By Delois Polk

HOW WE FEEL ABOUT THE THREE MISSING BOYS

The news just suddenly broke out as a shock. The people were scared and angry, saying "Why would any person want to take the lives of the three boys."

The people in the country were scared and some were even scared to come to town. I feel sorry for those boys and I think they should be found. The missing boys were a shock to some. The white wasn't so sad.

They found their station wagon. It was burned. Some people think they are dead. Some say the police are not looking as hard as they should be and most people think they cut them up in little pieces and threw them in the river.

By Frances Lee Jeffries

Masthead of the Holly Springs *The Freedom News*.
Courtesy of the Wisconsin Historical Society.

have to give up their precious time and come here to help us and we know that they are here because of love. Love not only for us, but also because they love the United States. They know that before the United Stares can have the respect of other countries it must also have the respect of its own people, both Negro and white.

When we heard about the three freedom workers missing, we were hurt, but not shocked because many of our people have come up missing and nothing was said or done about it. Ever since I can remember I have been told of such cases from my people, but never have I heard it said on the news or over the T.V. or radio. This was known only to a few of us, not nation-wide. X Even though most of us have given up hope about the three freedom workers, we are praying they will be found alive.

The freedom workers have the blessings and prayers of the Negroes in Mississippi. We will be forever grateful.

By Dolois Polk

How We Feel about the Three Missing Boys

The news just suddenly broke out as a shock. The people were scared and angry, saying "Why would any person want to take the lives of the three boys."

The people in the country were scared and some were even scared to come to town. I feel sorry for those boys and I think they should be found. The missing boys were a shock to some. The white wasn't so sad.

They found their station wagon. It was burned. Some people think they are dead. Some say the police are not looking as hard as they should be and most people think they cut them up in little pieces and threw them in the river.

By Frances Lee Jeffries

Marshall County, Mississippi

Holly Springs is located in Marshall County. It is inhabited by 28,000 people of which 2/3 are Negro. The town of Holly Springs has a population of 5,321 people. Most of the Negroes in Marshall County live outside the town, and their main occupation is farming. The main crop is cotton.

Most of the farmlands and plantations are owned by the white men. On the farm there are two things to choose from: sharecropping or renting. On each farm the white man gives the Negro a share to occupy. While the Negro is working on the plantation, the white man gives the Negro a tractor, and in some places a mule, to plow with. Most of the houses on the farm are contaminated, but the county will not condemn them. Because they don't care about them.

The working conditions are bad. The wages are very low. The amount paid for plowing a tractor all day is three dollars.

The white man buys most of the supplies used for the annual crops, but the Negro contributes all the labor. Each fall of the year when the crop is harvested and the cotton is sold to the market, the white man gives the Negro what he thinks he needs, without showing the Negro a record of the income the white man has collected for the year. This process of farming has become a custom. This way of livelihood is not much different from slavery.

The town life of Holly Springs is also very bad. The wages of the Negroes range from 1.00 to 1.15 an hour with one exception, the school teachers, and they aren't paid very much. Anywhere a new Negro neighborhood is constructed it takes years before proper sewage lines are built. During this time they use private cesspools or outdoor toilets which contaminate the air in which we breathe. Some of the residents have neither private cesspools, outdoor toilets, nor proper sewage lines. This is also a menace to society. The Negro neighborhood has dirt roads in city limits.

Negro women can earn their livelihood as maids. She is paid a low wage for a large amount of work. For example, sometimes she walks to and from work. House cleaning, baby-sitting, washing, ironing, waxing floors, cooking three meals a day are part of her work. All for the low, low sum of two dollars a day.

The Negroes of Holly Springs have no recreation center. We have one park but it has been condemned because of hookworms. The city has done nothing to build the Negroes a new one. And the white man wonders why there are so many Negro children wandering around the corners and poolroom. Why? Because they have no other place to go.

The white school is far better equipped than the Negro school. We have overcrowded classrooms and lack many subjects which should be taught in high school. The W. T. Sims High School is uncredited by the State of Mississippi.

And this is what the white man calls democracy for the Negroes.

By Roy DeBerry, Jr.
And Herman Ivy, Jr.

◆ ◆ ◆

July 10, 1964

Nov. 22, 1963

By Arelya J. Mitchell

The day was still and sad.
And in my little town it was
Windy, dark, and wet.

The day went on and on so slow.
Oh, how I wished it would end!
Then it came on the radio,
That the President had been shot.
"Shot!," said I.
"Shot!," said I, "Oh no, that can't be true!"
But in the emergency room they tried their
Might to save him, but the hope was slowly
Dying away as the afternoon began to fade
Promptly away.
Everyone just stopped and prayed. Their
Hearts skipped thump after thump as their
Throats began to lump (with tears).
Then the radio began to speak,
"He's dead. The President of the United
States is dead."

All was still.
All was sad. A thunderbolt had hit our path.
Eyes fell down.
Tears fell down.
No one made a joyful sound.

A knot curled in my throat—
A knot that seems to have not been broken.
That phrase had hit us as if in answer to
our prayers.
Why an answer so deep and sad?
Why an answer that has not a care?
All these questions and not any answers to me
Or no one else but Thee.
The next day was different—
As different can be for the flag
Was lowered at half staff, you see.
All that happened the other day seemed to have been but a
dream.
Some believing.
Some unbelieving.
Some just staring and looking.
This was the date the world cried.
This was the date the world stood still.
This is the date we'll never forget!

Freedom Training School

Freedom Training School is designed for the young as well as old.
Here we learn. Here we study history, we sing and do many more
interesting things.

Here we are trained to become better citizens of our town,
state, and country. We talk about the condition of Holly Springs:
the jobs for the Negroes and the living conditions.

Freedom Training School is a great help to the Negro Society of Mississippi. If we join together we can make this School a

success. So let's learn to be better citizens of our town. And help all better Americans.

By Gussie Brettle

Hopes and Fears

The Negroes of Mississippi think their prayers are finally being answered. We have waited and prayed so long for the day when we could get a job in any factory that is in need of employees, go to any restaurant we would like to eat at, or sit on any seat on the bus that we chose.

Some of us are afraid to speak and do the things we think would help Mississippi. We are afraid because of our jobs, our children's lives, etc. We have heard over radios and T.V. about some of the Negroes that tried to help Mississippi. For example, Medger Evers who was the Field Secretary of the NAACP and also a great leader. And the three freedom workers that are missing. The Negroes of Mississippi are praying that God has spared their lives and that they will soon be found alive.

By Ira Moore

IMPORTANT: The <u>Freedom News</u> will be published as often as possible throughout the summer. Everyone is welcome to write for the paper on any subject whatsoever. If you want to write an article or if you have written something that you would like to have printed, speak to one of the COFO workers about it.

◆　◆　◆

The Freedom News (Holly Springs, MS)

July 14, 1964

Why the Negro of Mississippi Should Vote

The Negro of Mississippi should vote so that he may get the thing he wants in life as a citizen of Mississippi and the United States of America.

Some of us sit around and say "I wish I could have things that the white man had: for instance, houses, proper sewage, better schools, roads, and most of all better jobs."

Some say, "Mr. Charlie has a good asphalt street leading to his house. My street is nothing but sand. If a rain comes you can't even get to my house, but a flood can come and you can still get to Mr. Charlie's house." His children get a very good education here in Mississippi. Why can't your children do the same thing or get better jobs.

You may say, "If I vote I may leave my job." What will you lose? Not anything. Do you want to do all the hard work and get the lowest wages all your life? Of course not.

Some of us work for 1.15 to 1.25 an hour. This is about the highest we can get in Mississippi. The white man, gets 3 or 4 times as much.

So don't sit around and say "I wish" all the time. If the Negro as a whole would go to the polls and vote he would have the things he wants and wouldn't have to wish for it.

God helps those who help themselves. So help yourself and go up and vote today. Tomorrow may be too late.

By Gary Phillip Faulkner

What Would You Do?

I'm pretending I'm a white businessman in Mississippi. The business I own is the only means I have to make a decent living for my family. My business is getting along just fine so far, and so is my family life. In my particular business I need men to do some of the work. I'm not prejudiced against Negroes, therefore I'll hire Negroes also and pay them the same as I pay my white workers.

Everything is O.K. until a phone call saying, "If you don't get rid of the niggers we will run you out of business." Now I'm upset. What should I do? The Negroes are my friends and their work is excellent. I hate to turn against them. Will they understand? What can I say? If I keep them, my own family that I love so much will suffer nor is it right for the Negro to suffer. I'm not rich so I can't establish a business someplace else. All of my money is invested in this one. I love my family more than anything else in the world, therefore they come first.

I called my Negro workers together and explained the situation. Bless them, they understood. I payed each one of them and told him that if he needed anything to let me know. I would do all I could without endangering my loved ones. I know I could have helped the Negroes if only I knew more businessmen who feel as I do. Together we would have won this battle, but who are they? Where are they? How would I go about finding them?

By Dolois Polk

Let's Take a Look

I hear that Mayor Sam Coopwood of Holly Springs, Mississippi, has asked Methodist Bishop Marvin Franklin of Jackson, Miss., to investigate Rust College and Dr. Ernest Smith, its president. My! Things are getting touchy, aren't they?!

He also wrote a letter dated June 29 to Bishop Franklin. The letter: "The good people of Holly Springs, both white and colored, are very much disturbed about the activity at Rust College."

"As you probably know there are about 100 white and colored students from Oxford, Ohio, and other parts of the country living on the Rust Campus." (Now get this) "White boys and girls are living together with the colored."

Then he goes on to say, "As Mayor of Holly Springs and as a member of the official board of the Methodist Church, I respectfully request that you and your group investigate Dr. Smith and Rust College.

Well! Let's go back. He says he's a member of the Methodist Church. I wonder if he believes all men are created equal. If he does I wonder what could be so bad about colored and white living together? I wonder if he can answer that question. As Booker T. Washington said and I quote, "You can't keep a man in the hole without being down yourself." Don't you think that kind of fits Mayor Coopwood? While he's trying to keep the Negro down he's really lowering himself and Mississippi!! (That fits a lot more Southern States too.)

Most people in Holly Springs (and other places too) aren't quite citizens—not excepting the whites. The colored people aren't quite citizens because they don't vote and some don't try to vote! The white people aren't quite citizens because if they were they'd accept the Bill of Rights. So see, we're even. Why deep fighting things back? You've got to take the medicine sometime or other, so why not take it now?

By Arelya J. Mitchell

◆ ◆ ◆

July 17, 1964

I was out canvassing one day trying to get my freedom registration forms filled. I had been working hard all day trying to get them filled, but I hadn't had any luck. I finally decided to go to the housing project and I came to the man's house named John. At first I started talking to his wife, but I wasn't getting anywhere with her. She just came right out and said she wouldn't sign for me or anyone else, because she didn't have time. Then her husband walked into the room and I started talking to him but he said right away he didn't have time to think about what I was saying because he had more important things on his mind. I asked him what was more important that what we were trying to do.

I said, "That's why Negroes aren't getting anywhere in the world today, because they don't have time for something that will help them, but they can always find time for what Mr. Joe or Mrs. Sue say. Why can't we seem to find time for something that will help our race?"

After I said that, he just stared at me for a while, and then he said, "I just haven't the time."

I just stood there wondering why he kept saying, "I don't have the time," because all he was doing was just sitting there doing nothing and yet he couldn't find time for something he needed. I wrote his name and address down as I walked away and kept wondering, "why . . . why?

By Dorothy Louise Lucas

Don't Care

While out canvassing one day, I stopped in on Mrs. Jones. I asked her to fill in a registration form so that she would be able to vote.

"Well honey," she said, "I don't think I would care to vote."

I asked, "Why wouldn't you care to vote?"

She said, "Why should I? My vote wouldn't make any difference whatsoever. Just my one vote: How could it help?"

I said, "Why of course it would help. It can make a lot of difference. Your one vote could make the person you vote for win by one vote, maybe even break a tie. If you did vote you could even say you have some voice in the government."

Then she said, "Well, I will think about it and you come back tomorrow and I'll give you my answer."

By Bonnie Tidwell

Satisfied

I took my registration form applications for registration to vote and went out. I met this lady coming down the street. I said, "Good evening."

She said, "Hello."

I said, "How are you?"

She said, "Fine, and you?"

I said, "I'll do. I'm just tired."

Then I said, "I'm from Holly Springs Freedom School, and I would like to ask you a few questions."

Then she just looked at me and said, "They have already been to me and I will tell you like I told them. I have a home, a family, and everything I could possibly want." And she just walked off.

I wouldn't let things go at that so I caught up with her, and explained everything to her and asked some more questions.

But all she said was, "Things stand as before. I'm sorry, try someone else."

It really made me mad. But then I thought a while and tried to understand her. Probably she was accustomed to letting other people think or talk for her. And if she did register to vote she could lose what she had. That is possible down South, you know.

By Edma Mary Schols

The Local News

This is a brief preview of the Freedom School here in Holly Springs, Mississippi. The classes that they are teaching here are in French, Art, English, Religion, History, Biology, Dancing, and the names of some of the teachers are Peter, Sandra, Bettina. Etc. My teacher that teaches me dancing practices with us the different things you can do with your waist, legs, fingers, arms, and body.

In my art class we learn how to sketch the eye, mouth, hand, and face.

Yesterday we learned how to sketch Moses holding the Bible. The outside people are wondering what it is like to be going to Freedom School. Well, this is my opinion: we are one big happy family and I think that is the way we will be forever. This is to you people that are talking about being afraid to attend the Freedom School and afraid to register and vote: you are missing one of the most important parts of your life. This is to you parents, especially you that are talking about the fact that you have children: you should talk this over and come to a decision and stand up and be counted as citizens of today's world.

Tuesday night there was a mass meeting held at Chulahoma Church. The meeting started at 7:30 PM. They had about 150 members at this meeting.

By Mavis J. Farrow

Freedom's Journal (McComb, MS)

With the help of local activists including NAACP members C. C. Bryant and E. W. Steptoe, McComb was one of the first places where SNCC gained a foothold. The McComb Freedom's Journal helps demonstrate the importance of African American history to the Freedom School students. As in other schools across the state, McComb Freedom School students were anxious to position themselves within the longer African American freedom struggle and honor black heroes from the past. As explained in this issue of the Freedom's Journal, McComb Freedom School students named their paper after America's first black newspaper, which was originally published in New York City in 1827. Although the editors of the McComb paper inaccurately credited Richard Allen as the editor of the original Freedom's Journal (the first editors were actually John B. Russwurm and Samuel Cornish), they clearly wanted to pay homage to the pioneering African American publication. Besides adopting the name of the nation's first black newspaper, the producers of the McComb Freedom School newspaper also modeled their cover illustration after the classic abolitionist symbol "Am I Not a Man and a Brother?" Their attention to black history is evident throughout each issue of this newspaper.

McComb Freedom School students were significantly impacted by their community's short but powerful tradition of youth activism. As one of the first SNCC projects in Mississippi, McComb was home to a courageous group of young African Americans who in 1961 had staged a walkout of their city's Burglund High School after fellow student Brenda Travis was expelled for trying to integrate a local bus stop. This highly visible and courageous protest helped set the tone for future youth activism and three years later continued to influence McComb Freedom School students. One of the veterans of the 1961 Burglund walkout, Curtis Hayes, even wrote a guest essay in an issue of the McComb Freedom's Journal. The essays and poems published in this newspaper illuminate the ways McComb Freedom School students were claiming leadership *roles in their community and even challenging older residents who they felt were not active enough.*

July 24, 1964

Dedication

We are naming our newspaper <u>Freedom's Journal</u> in honor of Reverend Richard Allen. He was editor of the first Negro newspaper and we are proud to borrow from him the name of that paper. We have in mind Allen's plans to help solve the problem of slavery in America.

We feel the need to continue the work done by this great man because: too long the public has been deceived by the aims of many American organizations; too long the things that rightfully belong to us are not given; too long others have done our speaking for us.

It is our earnest wish to express our true feelings about Mississippi and its people in our journal.

Dorothy Brown

Isn't It Awful?

Isn't it awful not to be able to eat
in a public place
Without being arrested or snarled at
right in your face?
Isn't it awful not to be able to go to
a public library and get an interesting book
Without being put out and given a
hateful look?
Isn't it awful not to be able to sleep
peacefully nights
For fear you may get bombed because

you want your rights?
Isn't it awful not to be able to get
your schooling where you please?
Just because of our race, color and
creed we cannot feel at ease.

Edith Moore

Freedom's Journal

Editor: Barbara JoAnn Lea
Editors of the week: Dorothy Vick, Edith Moore, Jacqueline Nobles.
Staff Members: Bernell Eubanks, Thelma Eubanks (cover), Georgia Patterson, Sandra Thompson, Gloria Jackson, Paula Moore, Steve Sephus, Sue Sephus, Dorothy Brown, Marionette Travis, Melvin Carter, Donald Tate, and others.

Ministers and Freedom Project

There used to be a time when Negro Mississippians were filled with doubt as to whether other people from other places cared enough to help them. From our talk with the Rev. Don McCord and the Rev. Harry Bowie we now know differently.

When asked about FREEDOM in Miss. the Rev. Bowie stated that "a man who isn't free is a man who is dead. He is like a robot: he moves, walks, talks and breathes, but still he is dead."

Rev. McCord made a comparison between Berlin and Mississippi. He said, "Berlin is a city with a wall through it and the people cannot visit from one side to the other. In Mississippi a wall has been built up by terror, intimidations, beatings, and bombings." He also stated that it's time to tear down the walls to show that people can live together in peace and harmony.

Rev. Bowie was asked about the three missing civil rights workers. He said that their actions encouraged him to come to Mississippi. The Rev. McCord felt that "the three missing workers made me realize for the first time how serious the situation is.

People from the outside are needed to make the whole country start to watch and see what has been going on in Mississippi for a long, long time."

Marionette Travis

Weekly Quotation

"So long as one man is chained, no one is free."

Rousseau (we think)

THE FREEDOM DEMOCRATIC PARTY WILL SOON BE HOLDING PRECINCT MEETINGS. PLEASE TRY TO ATTEND.

The House of Liberty

I came not for the fortune, nor for fame,
I seek not to add glory to an unknown name,
I did not come under the shadow of night,
I came by day to fight for what's right.
I shan't let fear, my monstrous foe,
Conquer my soul with threat and woe.
Here I have come and here I shall stay,
And no amount of fear my determination can sway.

I asked for your churches, and you turned me down,
But I'll do my work if I have to do it on the ground,
You will not speak for fear of being heard,
So crawl in your shell and say, "Do not disturb."
You think because you've turned me away
You're protected yourself for another day,

But tomorrow surely must come,
And your enemy will still be there with the rising sun;
He'll be there tomorrow as all tomorrows in the past,

And he'll follow you into the future if you let him pass.
You've turned me down to humor him,
Ah! Your fate is sad and grim,
For even tho' your help I ask,
Even without it I'll finish my task.

In a bombed house I have to teach my school,
Because I believe all men should live by the Golden Rule.
To a bombed house your children must come,
Because of your fear of a bomb,
And because you've let your fear conquer your soul,
In this bombed house these minds I must try to mold,
I must try to teach them to stand tall and be a man.
When you, their parents, have cowered down and refused to
make a stand.

Joyce Brown

The Golden Rule

The Freedoam School is nice and neat,
Everything is awful sweet.
Every day we jump and sing,
Thanking God for everything.

Every time I go to school,
I always keep the Golden Rule,
So if you go to the Freedom School,
Please don't forget the Golden Rule.

Stephanie Nobles
age 12

Freedom's Journal (McComb, MS)

Lawyers Help in Fight for Freedom

During this fight for the Negroes' freedom and liberty, lawyers, both Negro and white have been sent to Miss. from the north to take affadavits to show discrimination toward the Negro workers.

Clint Hopson, a Negro law student presently working in the state, says that he was sent here to work with COFO. He has worked with other civil rights organizations as well. Clint said that this is not his first time in the South.

"I feel," stated Mr. Hopson, "that this is my fight as well as anybody else's, and I intend to do as much as possible to help by doing whatever I can in any way I can."

Paula Leona Moore

The Freedom Train

The Freedom Train is coming, coming, coming, coming,
The Freedom Train is coming,
And we'll all get aboard.

There's Sally, Jane, and Tom,
There's our Freedom teachers,
One, two, three, and four,
Five, six, seven, and more.

Deborah Ann Watson
age 11

Opinion: The Way to Freedom

We are accustomed to say that the truth makes us free. It does nothing of the kind. It is the knowledge of the truth that creates freedom. "Ye shall know the truth and the truth shall make you free." We are now at the stage where the main emphasis must be laid on the dissemination of the truth. We need, as we have never before needed, a Campaign of Education. Freedom, to a great extent, depends upon our potentials and our horizons. Sometimes we feel that we are free only because we are satisfied with our limited achievements, goals, aspirations. As Jefferson stated, "We hold these truths to be self-evident: that all men are created equal; that they are endowed by their Creator with certain unalienable rights; and that among these rights are life, liberty, and the pursuit of happiness."

Thelma Eubanks

Harriet Tubman: A Brief Biography (1823–1913)

She was born on the eastern shore of Maryland, a slave property. Harriet was not cut out for slavery at all.

As she grew into her teens and got married, she began to think of a way to escape. She asked her husband, sister and brother to come with her, but none of them did. Her mind was made up, though, and she successfully escaped to Philadelphia. There she got a job and was free, but she still was not satisfied. Harriet wanted to help her relatives and friends escape from slavery. She did just that, by way of the Underground Railroad. Making nineteen trips back to the South, Harriet freed more than three hundred slaves.

After riding-in all the people she could, Harriet settled down. She was given a small pension of $20 a month on which she died poor, but great.

Dorothy Vick

Don't Weep

Oh, Negro of the America,
Why doth thou weep so?
Is it because you are from Africa?
Are you afraid of what you know?

Freedom's Journal (McComb, MS)

My "Granny" always told me
(of course she's passed on now)
That Negroes could be what they want to,
No matter what or how.
She told me of the Africans,
Captured by the Whites;
Brought to the Americas
Through they knew it wasn't right.
Work on fellow Negroes!
And get your equal rights.
I am there beside you,
For we all, we all must fight.

E. Le Verne Moore

Voter Registration Moving Nicely

Attempts to get people to register to vote for regular elections as well as for Freedom Registration are proving successful.

As a Freedom Registration worker, Freddie Green of COFO stated, "Freedom Registration is a form of challenging the Democratic Party." She said that through Freedom Registration it is hoped that we will be able to send some Negro representatives from Mississippi to the National Democratic Convention.

Miss Green feels that Freedom Registration is one way of getting people to help themselves. It also shows that Mississippi Negroes do care about their future.

If you haven't registered for Freedom Registration, forms can be obtained from the Freedom House, 702 Wall Street.

Edith Moore

ONE ONE
   X
MAN VOTE

McComb Freedom Fighter

Curtis E. Hayes, a local civil rights worker, lived in McComb from 1944–1961, and graduated from Eva Harris High School (Brookhaven) as salutatorian of his class.

After finishing high school, Hayes went to Wisconsin where he got job making $1.75 an hour. Previously he had earned $2.00 a day working evenings after school, and $4.00 a day working summers in Mississippi.

The community in which Curtis lived had two Negro families, although segregation was practiced in this part of Wisconsin. His roommate who was white, often asked Curtis what he had done to help his race. After repeatedly being questioned on this issue, Curtis decided that he would return to Mississippi and learn all that he could about the civil rights movement and about what he could do to help.

When Curtis returned home toward the end of the summer of 1961, he managed to meet Robert Moses and discuss the movement with him.

After talking to Moses, Curtis decided to spend the remaining part of the summer working in the movement, and then begin the fall semester at Jackson State College. But by the beginning of the semester he had been arrested, and because of the arrest he was not accepted at school.

After JSC refused to admit him, Curtis continued to work in the movement. While working for civil rights, Curtis has been arrested some ten times and has spent about one hundred twenty days in jail. He has been jailed in McComb, Jackson, Greenville, Indianola, Greenwood, and Ruleville. Curtis has organized voter registration projects throughout the state.

Barbara Jo Ann Lea

SOMEONE FROM McCOMB IS GOING TO ATTEND THE DEMOCRATIC NATIONAL CONVENTION IN AUGUST. IT MAY BE YOU! <u>DON'T FORGET TO FREEDOM REGISTER</u>

Some Thoughts on Freedom

FREEDOM is going to the public libraries.
FREEDOM is eating in any public place.
FREEDOM is standing up for your rights.
FREEDOM is attending schools of your choice.
FREEDOM is having a voice in your government.
FREEDOM is racial equality, justice and fraternity.
FREEDOM is happiness for all.
FREEDOM is being able to voice your opinion.
FREEDOM is attending a church of your choice.
FREEDOM is making use of public recreational facilities.
FREEDOM is being able to think for yourself; being able to
form your own opinion.
FREEDOM is the right to publish fact and opinion without
censorship.
FREEDOM is . . .

You're Free to Laugh

Tom: Why shouldn't you tell a secret in a garden?
Dianne: Because the corn has ears.

Zachary Patterson
age 12

◆　◆　◆

August 11, 1964

Editor
Barbara JoAnn Lea

Editors of the Week
Sue Scolaus
Marilyn Sarter
Viola Williams

Cover
Thelma Eubanks

Freedom's Journal is a published weekly (or thereabouts) in McComb, Mississippi. Comments and articles from all readers are most welcome. See us at the Freedom House or else mail material care of this paper [indecipherable].

A Word from the Editors

The editorial board takes this space to praise the Negro youth of McComb for a splendid job in helping the Freedom Movement of this town. The Negro Youths have proved that they are willing to help their race in any way that they can. They have attended the Freedom School and helped the workers in every way they could.

But many of the adults in McComb are a great disappointment to their race. Some will not let their children attend Freedom School because they are afraid. They will not even Freedom Register. A few adults, like their children, will support their race in every way they can.

Very few people are playing an active part in the civil rights movement. They want their rights but don't want to fight for them. Therefore the younger generation is doing more for the Summer Project than most adults in our community.

The students have helped by canvassing for Freedom Registration and also by passing out leaflets. They have also helped by attending Freedom School every day and participating in the daily classes. They also helped by convincing others to attend Freedom School.

If only the adults of the community would wake up and see what they are really doing to their children by keeping them at home, the Summer Project in McComb would probably be the most successful in the state.

The older people, who should be most willing to cooperate in any way possible, are often the most uncooperative in the community. If someone would make them realize that the people of COFO and the Freedom School teachers at the Freedom House are here only for their benefit and for the benefit of their children and that without their full cooperation the complete success of the Summer Project is impossible. As Frederick Douglas once said, "If there is no struggle, there is no progress."

An Interview

Two White Mississippi college students were interviewed about the happenings in McComb. Their main reason for making their appearance at the Freedom House was to see Pete Seeger, and the other reason was just out of curiosity, to see what was going on. They didn't mind being interviewed by a Negro girl because, as one of them stated, "It doesn't make any difference what race you are," and he had never been interviewed before.

The boys were asked if they were for integration. One of them answered, "Definitely." They said that the presence of civil rights workers in McComb is good, worthwhile but that the proper tactics are not being employed. They do feel that the workers could be making progress.

One of them had this to say: "The white people of McComb are dead set against the workers being here. The whites think that the Negro is satisfied with the present system. The Negroes as individuals in the southern states are just great, but as a race they are not so great. The whites feel just the opposite in the North.

The boys felt most elections are a waste of time, that they accomplish nothing. As for the voting test, the boys think that improper ones are given to the whites. The whites have simple tests which only take a few minutes, and the Negro is given a longer improper test. Some whites who are not educated still vote.

One of the boys argued that southern Negroes should be trained up North and then sent back down here to teach the people what the northerners are now teaching then. Should this be done, all of the tenseness would disappear.

As for the Freedom Democratic Party, the boys did not think very much of it. They think that all efforts put forth by the Negro should be made in the regular Mississippi Democratic Party.

Thelma Eubanks

Sojourner Truth—A Brief Biography

Mrs. Truth was born as Isabella Baunfreo about 1797, the property of a Dutch nester in New York. Mrs. Truth spoke English all her life. She lived with her parents. Then one day Isabella's parents died, and she was sold and resold.

She became the property of John Dumont, in whose service she remained until New York State freed its slaves in 1827. When the state freed its slaves, Isabella's master did not grant her to go, but she ran away and left her children behind. Then one day she heard that when her son, Pete, was five he was sold. Instead of going on to be free, she went to court to get her son back, and she succeeded.

Mrs. Truth went to court again. This time she was accused of the murder of a white man, but there was not enough proof to convict her. She sued for libel and won a judgment of $125, which was unusual vindication for a Negro then.

In the year of 1843 Isabella decided to leave her job as a domestic servant in order to travel. She said that, "the spirit called me," and "I must go." The Lord gave her the name of Sojourner Truth. She was called Sojourner "because I was to travel up and down the land showin' the people their sins and bein' a sign unto them; Truth because I was to declare Truth unto the people."

Mrs. Truth became a famous figure of anti-slavery meetings. Once she said about her work, "I think of the great things of God, not the little things." Once a man told her that he cared no more about her work than he cared about a flea bite. "Maybe not," she replied, "but the Lord willin', I'll keep you from scratchin.'"

Viola Williams

Freedom's Journal (McComb, MS)

When I Went to Vote

I went to the courthouse
To try an' vote.
My name was asked first
So that's what I wrote.

They asked me for my address
So I wrote that too,
(What else would you expect
For a fellow to do?)

I wrote my telephone number,
Also my description
Then I went on to fill out
The rest of the application.

It said for me to tell
What the Constitution said
So I did that and went ahead.

I answered the questions
From that one to the last,
But when they read my paper
They said I didn't pass.

But I didn't let that stop me
For I'm goin' back again,
'Cause I've got a funny feelin'
That this battle I'll surely win!

Paula Leona Moore

One Way to Deal with Strange Men on Your Property

Three country men were trying to figure out what to do when strange white men search around their property by night.

Sam—Well, I'm tellin' you, if I see dem rascals aroun' my place, I'm gonna shoot first an' ask questions later.

Buck—Sam, don't kill 'em; just round 'em. Have pity for 'em.

Rocomo—I think Buck is right, so I'll just shoot 'em in their legs. If they try to get away, I'll shoot 'em in their arms. Then I'll go outside and look those rascals straight in their eyes, and then I'll say I'm sorry.

Gloria Jackson

Weekly Quotation

"I had reached the point at which I was not afraid to die. This spirit made me a freeman in fact, though I still remained a slave in form."

Frederick Douglas

Dr. William Edward Burghardt DuBois (1868–1963)

Dr. DuBois was considered one of the great Campaigners. His great ambition was to go to Harvard College. His mother wasn't able to send him to Harvard. He worked in the summer hoping that he would make enough money to go to school. As it turned out he went to Fisk, where he met other people like himself. A grant was made to him from Fisk to go to Harvard for two years. After receiving his Bachelor's degree, he spent two more years in graduate school.

DuBois taught many subjects including a rather new one, sociology. At the school where he was teaching, he met his future wife. The death of their first born son hurt them deeply.

There were great differences between DuBois and Booker T. Washington on matters of policy and program for the uplift of the Negro people in the United States. In an address to the Cotton States Exposition in Atlanta, Mr. Washington proposed a compromise by which the Negro would not ask for social or political equality in return for a pledge that he would be provided with industrial training and the opportunity to take a place in the rapidly expanding economy of the nation, then engaging in a period of post war boom. Mr. Washington's proposal was accepted with relief by the South and with enthusiasm by the North, where wealthy industrialists worked together to put funds into the Negro institutions designed to fulfill his limited objective. DuBois declared, in contrast, that while this might be a necessary move for the moment, the results would prove disastrous.

When the announcement of the death of Dr. DuBois was made, everything was silent. A woman cried out, "He's just like Moses."

Precethia Rollins

Hope

Sometimes I wonder if we are alone
If there is no one who will help us
Along.
We have fought and waited for Freedom
To appear.
But we are not alone
And our hearts are not filled with fear.

Somewhere I know there are people who
Care;
Freedom was meant for everyone, as it
Can only be.
The day that we get Freedom a new life
Will begin,
Our hearts will be joyful and with
Rapture will spin.

When we find Freedom, we will not let
It go,
And day by day our struggle will
Grow.

We can't always tell what happened in
The past,
But when we get Freedom, we know it
Will last.

But when will Freedom be here at our
Side?
Within its rights we are longing to
Bide.
Yes, we've struggled and waited for
Freedom to appear,
But still we are not alone and
Our hearts are not filled with fear.

Marionette Travis

Opinion—Freedom With Prejudice?

Freedom is as much a state of mind as it is a physical condition. No man can truly be free if the barriers of prejudice and disrespect are present, even if you are allowed to go where you wish. If this is given with reluctance and you are just put up with and not respected, you are not truly free. The seeds of prejudice that have been planted for a lifetime cannot be wiped out overnight. We must have time and patience and hope.

Anonymous

The Pete Seeger Story

On the 3rd of this month we had a world famous folk singer, Pete Seeger, visit us here in McComb. He has visited over 24 foreign countries. Seeger was born in New York State and raised in New England. He is married and has three children (one son, two daughters). His children attend an integrated school, and some of their closest friends are Negroes.

When asked why he is touring Miss., Seeger replied, "I am here because I want to see (and help) the Negroes win their fight for freedom, because 200 years ago my ancestors fought this same fight when they came over to America on the Mayflower. I also came because I feel I might encourage you to fight harder and because I also receive encouragement.

At the folk festival Pete sang such well-known songs as John Henry (which he wrote), Goodnight Gene (which he was the first to record), Tom Dooley, Oh Freedom and many other freedom songs.

Cofo is arranging Seeger's tour of Mississippi. He will visit Freedom Schools and churches all over the state. Seeger hopes to visit McComb again within a year or so.

We consider it an honor as well as a pleasure to have him begin his tour of Miss. by visiting the Freedom House and the McComb Freedom School

Seeger also said, "No man has ever had freedom handed him on a silver platter." So let us strive for the unity that we need to win our fight for freedom.

Barbara JoAnn Lea

Poem

I think the police know
The people who set bombs on your
window
But don't think it's only the white;
It's living proof of a Negro has been
inside
Now looking from my point of view
Considering Negroes it's only a few
Who would be lowdown enough
To be caught in that kind of stuff.
The police will tell you not to take
the law in your hand
But why wait to call when the bomb is

there and the person is off your
land?
It is wise to shoot or capture him
But don't get trigger-happy and shoot
Before you have enough proof.

N. S. S.

Book Review—The Negro Revolt

By Louis E. Lomax

On Dec. 1, 1955 Mrs. Rosa Parks, an attractive, middleaged woman, unintentionally started the Negro revolt. She did so by refusing to unseat herself from a bus seat so that whites could sit down, because of her aching feet.

The fact that the Negro has no secure identification has caused the revolt of today. Because of relationships with female slaves and white masters, Negroes have been deprived of their identity. In a sense, the American Negro is made by man and not God.

After the beginning of the revolt, organizations were established to help the Negroes advance. Some were the Southern Christian Leadership Conference (SCLC), the National Association for the Advancement of Colored People (NAACP), and the Congress of Racial Equality (CORE).

Four freshmen from the Agriculture and Technical College and Greensboro, North Carolina staged a sit-in in the local Woolworth dime store. When the news was heard on the local radio station, other students came to join. This started the second Negro revolt.

After that, many other sit-ins were staged. The techniques used were non-violence and mass action.

Another Negro organization was formed, the Student Non-Violent Coordinating Committee (SNCC), with Charles McDow presiding. SNCC is active in voter registration, freedom rides, and sit-ins.

On May 9, 1961, freedom rides were started to "test racial discrimination in interstate travel terminals." The rides began in

Washington and ended in New Orleans on May 17. At this point, others joined the freedom riders and began a series of rides which ended Nov. 1.

Some outstanding Negro leaders are Dr. King, originator of SCLC, James Farmer, program director of CORE, Marvin Rich, executive secretary of CORE, Roy Wilkins, executive secretary of NAACP, John Lewis, chairman of SNCC, Jim Foreman, executive secretary of SNCC, and Bob Moses, director of the Mississippi Project.

Mr. Lomax ended by saying, "Whatever the Negro is, he is American. Whatever the future awaits America, awaits the Negro. What future awaits the Negro, awaits America."

Edith Marie Moore

The '61 Walk-out

In 1961 a big step was made toward freedom and equality. It all started when a Negro girl, Brenda Travis, was not allowed to enter school because she has been active in civil rights demonstrations during the summer.

The morning she arrived at school we had assembly as usual. A committee was formed to ask the principal if Brenda would be admitted back to the school. The principal said, "Come down to the office and we'll see." This made the students angry, so about two-thirds of the students walked out.

After leaving the school they went to the Masonic Hall, where they met Bob Moses and other civil rights workers. There they printed posters. Their next step was to go down to the courthouse. After arriving there, a prayer was offered, and then another. On the way down a few people were beaten, but not seriously. After the students prayed and sang, the police came and said, "You are all under arrest."

The students gave their names and were then put in the jail cells. Then they told the jailer that they were hungry. Food and sodas were sent down. Next they asked for a broom and they cleaned up.

Later in the evening the students and civil rights workers were asked questions, such as: "Did you know what you were doing?" All the replies were "Yes." The next question was, "Aren't you taught to say 'Yes Sir?'" "Only to people we respect." Then those persons under 18 years were released and the rest were brought to the county jail in Magnolia.

Again the students returned to school, but some of the teachers and the principal wanted to know what they wanted there. So again they left. Many went to Campbell College, some quit school and other entered Burglund again.

Because of these demonstrations, the "colored" and "white" signs were removed from the train station and bus station.

Dorothy Vick

More Beatings

The story you are about to read is true, every word of it. The true name or names of the persons are not revealed to protect the innocent. This is the way the story was told to us by the person it happened to:

"It was about 9:30 and I was making the beds when I heard these two car doors slam. When the men who got out of the car called for me to come out, I ran to another room. But they kicked the front door down. It was about ten of them. They dragged me out to the car and put a rope around my neck and a black hood over my face. When I asked what they were going to do with me, one of them said, "Damnit, you'll find out." We drove about 12 miles on a paved road and then turned off on a dirt road and stopped. My hands were tied and the hood and rope were still around my neck. I heard water running, so I gave myself up for dead. But they just beat me and left me there. They jerked the rope from around my neck, which left two scars. Those are the only ones that can be seen. When I got to the highway, I didn't know which way to go. I decided to go East. I walked about three-fourths of a mile when I came to this house, where I stayed over night. When I returned, I moved in with my son, until I found a place to rent.

I owned my own home and land. It wasn't a palace but it was home and it had all the modern conveniences inside—water and bathroom. Now I'm living in this rented house with no running water inside. The bathroom doesn't work, and when you're used to something it's kind of hard to do without it.

Now that I am out here (this person once lived in Amite County and now lives in McComb) I still don't feel safe. I have ten kids and eight with the two older kids away. And I can't go back to my own home.

I myself think that the sheriff had a bit to do with it because he did not do anything about it, and he also told my son that if he knew I was back he would run me out himself. I think that the people of that county should be made to support me and my family until I get back to my own home."

Let's remember that this story is true. The only way the Negroes of Mississippi can stop this sort of thing is by sticking together and crawling out of those shells they are in and get on the ball and do something about it; that's the only way.

Billy Givens

Negro History Quiz

1. George Washington praised my poetry.
2. I was an American born actor (1807–1867), but I was an actor who never came home.
3. The old slaves considered me the Moses of my people.
4. I was a great Negro physician in my time.
5. A painting I painted now hangs in the Luxembourg.
6. I was considered the Robert Burns of Negro poetry.
7. I am the father of the blues.
a. Henry Turner
b. Harriet Tubman
c. Phyliss Wheatley
d. W. C. Handy

e. Paul Lawrence Dunbar
f. Ira Alridge
g. Daniel Hall Williams
<u>Turn Page Upside Down for Answers</u>
C, F, B, G, A, E, D

◆ ◆ ◆

August 24, 1964

A Word from the Editors

This summer in McComb a new Summer Project began. It was for the advancement of the young people and the adults as well.

It was called Freedom School. In Freedom School students are allowed to study any subject they would like, whereas in public schools you have to wait until you are in a particular grade to take a certain subject.

During this time, we have learned about ourselves and our ancestors. For the first time some of us had the experience of getting along with people of another race. We have also learned how to overcome fear of another race.

Now the time has come for us to say goodbye to our teachers and many of the [indecipherable] people that we have met while attending Freedom School. We are very sorry that the summer project is almost over and would like to compliment our teachers for doing such a wonderful job. We feel it was nice meeting <u>y'all</u> and we hate to see you leave.

Weekly Quotation

"A man who is good enough to shed his blood for his country is good enough to be given a square deal afterward."

Theodore Roosevelt

A Letter from Curtis

My Fellow Soldiers,

It is not common for one little member of a large army to sit down and write to the rest of the members, and by some token it is not common for one member to possess such love, warmth, affection, sympathy, devotion, and all of the beautiful words that come short of my feelings for you.

I am writing this letter because I want you to understand that though I love you, and McComb will always be my home, I must leave to get one more tool to work with. This tool is education.

Please don't forget that for months and maybe years to come there will be many COFO workers here. They will stay as long as you need them. There have been many plans made for our community and I beg you not to let their work be in vain.

I was born and raised here. Many of your hands have helped spank me into what I am today; many of the Christians who now disagree with me helped teach me what I now believe; the white community made it necessary for me to work for 2–4 dollars a day; gave me a choice between a pitiful poor and a poor school; they took some of the color away when they raped my great-grandmothers. This, all of this, I am proud of, for it has made me strong and courageous enough to join the army for FREEDOM NOW!! Thus, in the words of one of our great writers (somewhat paraphrased), "McComb need not be ashamed of her product for what we produce will be here in its entirety. Escape it? She cannot, for I am Negro. I am the present, the past, and I'll make my future."

Finally I will say, and I want you to hear me and hear me good—I WILL RETURN! I am reminded of a few words I read in a book given to me by Bob Moses which I wish to share with you. "The plague, like most evils, has caught up everyone and everything, no longer are there individual destinies—only a collective destiny, and the emotions shared by all . . . We are hostile to the past, impatient with the present, and afraid of being cheated in the future . . . Heroism or sanctity doesn't really appeal to me—what interests me most I guess is being a man ... Love—exile—suffering." WE SHALL OVERCOME

Curtis Elmer Hayes

I Have Been to School

I have been to school in another state
Coming back to Mississippi was a big mistake.
The schools down here have very old books
If you don't believe me take a second look
This past term some of my books were as old as I
It's really something that no one should deny
Now coming to Mississippi for other reasons may be good
But coming for an education I advise that no one should
Even if the Mississippi schools had integration
I know the other states (especially up North) would provide a
better education
Some of you will try to interpret some of what I have said into
a lie
I don't think you can, but you are free to try.

Sue Sephus

Freedom School Convention

Friday, Aug. 7—Three delegates, Thelma Eubanks, Marionette Travis and Jessie Diven left McComb City to attend the Freedom School Convention in Meridian, Mississippi. On arrival at 6 P.M., they signed in. After getting their luggage packed away, they met with other delegates and marched to the memorial of James Chaney. After this they went to the school for assembly, and afterward they went to bed.

On the following day the delegates went back to the Meridian Freedom School at 9 A.M. for assembly. The devotion was led by different individuals. Then all sang freedom songs. Afterward the delegates were assigned to workshops where they made resolutions.

After they assembled and read all the resolutions that were passed. Almost all of the resolutions of McComb were passed.

On the next day the delegates went to church. Later, a service in the Freedom School was held. After this they talked about boycotts that were going on around the state. Then Bob Moses got up and asked the students their opinions about Freedom School. What did they like about it? What would they like to see continued? How would they like it to be continued? After Moses, other people spoke also.

The following day the delegates and leaders (among whom was Joyce Brown) had a meeting to choose delegates to go to the Democratic National Convention in Atlantic City, New Jersey. Thelma Eubanks was one of the delegates elected. She was also elected National Committeewoman. After the meeting, the delegates packed to come home.

Marilyn Carter

Some Thoughts about Freedom School

I want Freedom School to keep on.
I like everything about Freedom School.
I like art.
I like Freedom School.
I don't like to get up in the morning to come to Freedom
School.
I like for Helen to read stories in Freedom School.
I like my teacher in Freedom School.
I like my teacher in Freedom School.

Denise Ledbetter
I am ten years old

Freedom's Journal (McComb, MS)

A Prayer for Goldwater

Dear, O Heavenly Father
I do not wish anyone death
But please let Goldwater be thrown in with a cage of lions
If he don't die then let the ambulance that carries him to the hospital have four flat tires
If he don't die then let the food that he eats have ptomaine poisin in it
If he don't die then let the doctors that operate on him have gorillas on their backs
If he don't die then, please, let him be President.

From Time Magazine

A Story Continued from Our Aug. 3rd Edition

After the Ku Klux Klan found out that Cindilillia was colored, they brought her to trial. Everyone in the courthouse was a member of the Ku Klux Klan, including the judge. Cindilillia knew she was not getting a fair trial. She even tried to get a lawyer, but he said she was crazy. He asked her if she wanted him to get killed, so her hope for a lawyer was forgotten. But just as they were fixin to pass sentence, in walked Bobby Kennedy. He told them that Cindilillia was going to have a fair trial. Cindilillia had her fair trial. She was not convicted. After her trial she thanked Bobby Kennedy, sold her home and left the state of Mississippi never to return.

Janice Carstafhnur

How I Feel about the State of Miss.

The Constitution of Mississippi as a whole is very unfair. I mean that it is or rather it has very unfair laws. The lawmakers of Mississippi pass some very unfair laws. We have some unfair people running our government business. The police are not doing anything about Mississippi or the banks.

Julius Benton

Pike and McComb

There are 35,063 persons in Pike County, according to the official U.S. Census in 1960. This is 1964, and the number of persons in Pike may have changed greatly.

Of the 35,063 persons, 41.9% are Negroes, which means that about four of every ten persons in Pike County are Negroes and about six out of ten are whites.

In Pike County there are 8,417 families of which 5,333 are white and 3,084 are Negro. Half of all the families, Negro and white, in Pike County, have incomes above $3,213, and half of the families make less. Half of the Negro families in Pike make more than $1,800 per year and half make less than $1,800.

The number of Negro families which make less than $2,000 per year is 1,704. The number of Negro families which make less than $3,000 per year is 2,339.

The total population of McComb is 12,020 with 8,605 persons being white and 3,415 being Negro. In white families there are usually about three persons and in Negro families there are usually about four persons.

Marvin Carter

Why?

Why are we the underclass?
Why do we always get served last?
Better jobs and higher pay
The white man gets any day
Better schools and nice hotels
If we try to use them we'll be in jail

The white man has lunch counters galore
Yet we aren't allowed to use the drug store
But we are going to win our rights
Or we shall have a real big fight.

Gwendolyn Flowers

For the Last Time

For the last time take your foot off my neck and give me rights as a citizen. Don't single me out for special censure or special awards.

For the last time give me my rights as a citizen and a taxpayer in employment, education, housing, and public accommodations. Don't condescend to give me in charity what is really mine, under the laws of the land. Just let me live my life as a free and full citizen. That is all I ask.

L. B. C.

Uncle Thomas Learns a Lesson: A Story

Joey was a Negro boy who lived in the Northern part of Illinois. His best friend was Dave, a little white boy. Joey loved Dave and Dave loved Joey as if they were brothers, for you see, Joey had not a brother or sister and Dave had no sister, brother, mother, or father. For these reasons Joey and Dave came to mean a great deal to each other.

Dave lived with his Uncle Thomas, who had just moved to Illinois from the South, one month after the death of his brother. Uncle Thomas did not like anyone the color of Joey, and for this reason he demanded that Dave stop seeing Joey. To make sure that Dave did not see Joey, Uncle Thomas sent him to summer camp in the summer and to a private school in the winter.

Whenever Joey's parents came to ask Uncle Thomas to dinner or church, he would say very harshly, "go away, niggers." Soon all the people in the neighborhood disliked Uncle Thomas. They stopped even trying to be nice to him. Soon he had not a friend in the whole neighborhood.

Now it happens that Uncle Thomas was rather up in age and suffered with his heart. One day as he was working in the kitchen his heart began to hurt and the next thing he knew he was lying on the floor. Just then a knock came at the door; it was Joey. Since no one bothered to open the door, Joey decided to go away and leave the old man alone, never to be bothered by him again. "But then if I did this I would be just like Uncle Thomas, all of the hatred with no love at all," thought Joey. So he went to the door, opened it and went on in. A he stepped into the kitchen, there laying on the floor was Uncle Thomas with his hands over his heart. Joey immediately phoned the doctor, then his parents.

At the hospital, two weeks later, Dr. Jones told Joey's parents that "Mr. Thomas barely escaped death," and that it if was not for Joey, he would have probably died.

The next day Joey went to visit Uncle Thomas. As he stepped into the room, Uncle Thomas smiled at him for the first time.

"I hear you saved my life, boy," he said. "I'm mighty thankful."

Then he told Joey how sorry he was for the way he had treated him and how he was going to make it up to him and Dave. Then he began to cry. Joey moved closer to him and bent and kissed him on the cheek.

"Oh, that's all right, Uncle Thomas. Black people love white people, white people love black people. You just never learned until now. But me and Dave knew it a long time ago. If everyone would be like Dave and me, it would be a much better place to live."

N. W. C.

Now Is the Hour

Now is the hour
No other time will do

For us to go and get
What belongs to me and you

Now is the hour
To stand for what is right
Together we know
We will win the fight
Now is the hour
That we must say farewell
To tears and hardships
Freedom's better, I can tell

By: Edith Marie Moore

Some Interviews

<u>Mario Roberto Savio</u>—After a summer of working with the Miss. Summer Project, Mario plans to attend the University of California at Berkeley. "I have enjoyed this small start and if there is any possible chance, I hope to be back again next summer," said Mario. "The reason I came to the South was because I knew the Negroes down here were being denied the right to vote and I felt something should be done about it."

<u>Marshall Ganz</u>—A surprise to most people, but Marshall Ganz is staying down here this year. Says Marshall, "I came down here because I have been wanting to come here for a long time. One night, as you all know, crosses were burned, and I felt something should be done about it. Therefore, I left where I was working in the Summer Project and I came down to McComb. I think we have shown the people the handwriting on the wall."

Dorothy A. Vick

Freedom's Journal (McComb, MS)

Why Won't the White Man . . .

Why won't the white man let me be free?
Am I not a man as well as he?
Oh! If the Negro could only be free,
There'd be no race greater than we!

Of course there are folks who say, "We got what we deserve"
But these are the people who will always serve
They'll work long and hard with little pay
And never be thankful to see a new day

Oh! If the Negro could only see
How much he could do if he were free.
Oh! If the Negro would not only pray
But help in our fight for freedom and a brighter new day!

Barbara JoAnn Lea

Local Citizen Tells of Voting Test

Mrs. Lillian Ledbetter, wife of a prosperous Negro businessman, was one of the citizens to register to vote on Freedom Day.

Mrs. Ledbetter said that Freedom Day caused her to remember the right to vote was here and that she should take advantage of this right.

"I was not afraid," said Mrs. Ledbetter, "but I was in doubt as to what would happen after I got to the courthouse." She found that the registrar was not at all nasty. Mrs. Ledbetter had attended the citizenship class (which is still going on). Therefore, the test was very easy.

FBI agents were and still are on hand to protect prospective voters. Transportation is available if needed. Babysitters are also ready to serve you while you take the test.

Mrs. Ledbetter stated, "I would like for everybody to go register to vote. There is nothing, absolutely nothing to fear."

Edith Marie Moore

Fighting for Freedom

The thought of being free has entered many minds,
Most of the people are being left out or behind,
Very few people are willing to fight for what they believe is right,
But speaking for myself I'd rather fight day and night.
To win freedom we will have to fight,
This is how most people accomplished their rights.
But when I say fight I mean non-violently.
We will accomplish more that way.
This is the way that organization named SNCC works.
This is the way they believe freedom should be won.

P. R.

The Declaration of Independence

In the Declaration of Independence it said, "We hold these truths to be self-evident: that all men are created equal, that are endowed by their creator with certain unalienable rights; that among these rights are life, liberty, and the pursuit of happiness."

In a Negro's life he wants to know what does it mean by life, liberty, and the pursuit of happiness. The word <u>life</u> for a Negro means to live in fear all the time and work very hard to keep himself alive and his family with very small pay a week.

Liberty to him means that it's not for him but for the Caucasian man. Because he's not free to say what he wants when he wants to and how he feels about something. That's not liberty when you can't go home asleep at night without your home being bombed when you try to be like the white man.

The pursuit of happiness—we are not happy in a large way because we can't go to any public place and enjoy ourselves without somebody beating on us or pulling on us and saying everything to us. It's not happiness when we can't go to a public beach or movie, or a lunch counter to eat our dinner.

The Declaration of Independence says that all men are created equal. But we are not treated equally. So when will we be treated equally? The law was made July 4, 1776, and it is now all the same in 1964.

Georgia Patterson

Gideon Jackson's Hallelujah Song of Defiance

From <u>Freedom Road</u>

There ain't no grass grows under my feet
On Freedom road,
There ain't no grass grows under my feet
On Freedom road
Old John Brown, grand-daddy,
We're coming,
We're coming,
Down freedom road.

Howard Fast

Book Report: Freedom Road, By: Howard Fast

At the end of the Civil War and near the beginning of the Reconstruction period, freed negroes from a small village awakened and saw the men of the village returning home from voting. The children and women ran out to meet them. Gideon's wife, Rachel, didn't run out because she wasn't the type to do this. Many questions were asked about voting. They did not know what voting was because they hadn't heard of voting and never did any voting when they were slaves. Gideon Jackson answered most of the questions because his people looked up to him for many things. Gideon was selected as a delegate to a convention in Charleston. Each man went to his family giving them things they had bought back from the city.

Gideon was afraid to go to the convention because did not know how to read and write so well. Brother Peter told him not to be afraid; he would give him words that he knew how to write and told Gideon to buy a book and learn more.

Gideon did not know his parents. After having breakfast with Gideon and his family Brother Peter went out with Gideon and told him of the day that he was born. Gideon's mother died while giving birth to him. Brother Peter was made not to tell anyone of this.

Days later he received a letter from General E. R. S. Canby which contained papers he would need at the convention. Gideon's clothes were not for going to the convention. His friends gave him clothes and his wife sold them. With little food he started on his one hundred miles of walking, singing his hallelujah song.

He was treated badly by people such as Mr. Laits who was a former slave holder and who didn't believe that Negroes should go with such things as conventions. He also met James Allenby and his family, whom he spent the night with.

Mr. Allenby was an educated man. Gideon talked him into going to his home and teaching his family and friends.

When Gideon arrived in Charleston, he didn't have any money and he was tired. He worked for one day to get money to eat. Someone told him of the Carter's home where delegates were taken in. He lived here for two dollars a week.

Gideon read in the newspaper about the way people felt about Negroes. Men that Gideon met at the convention gave him a few books. Later, other delegates joined him in his studies. Gideon was invited to dinner at the home of Stephen Holms as the guest of honor. During the dinner, Gideon though that if women were not present, the men would kill him. After Gideon left, the other people talked angrily about how their plans had failed. One of the guests was a member of the Klan, and others invited to join it to go against the Negroes. They would get thousands of men in the Klan.

The state constitution was made, and it gave everyone life, liberty, and the pursuit of happiness. When it was time for Gideon to go, Mrs. Carter cried and kissed Gideon, because she and her husband had grown close to him. When he was near home, the children ran out to him. All of the people were glad to see him, to hear the things he had done and seen.

There was still a problem. They had no land. Gideon said they could borrow the money. Others said they could work on the railroad.

Gideon made plans for his son Jeff to go to Boston to study and learn to be a doctor.

Later people of the other village went to school.

The people worked and made money to pay for the mortgage on the land. But Carl Robbins, who was vice-president of the bank, would not take the money for the land. He said, "I don't approve of niggers owning land; spoils them."

Black codes were made to send the Negro back to slavery.

Gideon went to see President Grant to talk to him about his people. Grant would only be President for a few more days, but long enough to help the Negroes.

Jeff returned home at the age of 20 as Dr. Jackson. Soon everyone became afraid. They found out how the Klan worked. Ellen (blind daughter of Mr. Allenby) and Jeff wanted to get married. A man and his wife taken out of their home and beaten. The lady died and the man was hurt by the members of the Klan. Other members of the Klan came and burned the homes of the village and killed all the people.

Perceta Rollins

A Word to the Public

I think the Freedom School that has been organized in McComb is really nice. Because it has the most wonderful and understanding teachers you can find. I think that all the Negro families should allow their children to come to this wonderful school.

Listen, my fellow friends. It is time for you folk to wake up; you're letting yourself go astray. Wake up, people, and pull yourselves together before it's too late. You have a chance to get your freedom, you have a chance to change his myth about you that the white man has put out.

Do you want to make this myth seem as if it were true. Is that what you want? For God's sake, No! You want to be shown the way to the Freedom road but your afraid to ask for a guide for fear that you might get bombed, beaten, or killed. That's what's wrong with the Negro race today—they are afraid and won't pull together.

Remember what I said—wake up before it's too late and get a move on. You should have been letting your children come to Freedom School. They learn more in Freedom School than they do in public school because subjects such as Negro History are not taught in public school to kids. So remember, friends, there is no progress without struggle.

Brenda Allen

Everyone's Equal

If one would refer to the history of the Negro, he would see that it was not the Negro who insisted upon entering this vast country in which we now live. It was the Caucasian who invaded and captured the Negro and brought him to this country to work as a slave. It is not for the Caucasian to add to or detract from the intellect of a man.

Moving up on the ladder, we see where the Negroes were treated more and more cruelly than the lowest animal. During the time of the Emancipation Proclamation, people still wanted to ignore the Negroes purpose in life.

And the Caucasoids evolved an image of high society around the idea of white supremacy. The Caucasoids, supposed to be the high class groups, are still stupid and foolish enough not to see their brothers around them.

Yes, we the Negroes are their brothers. But have our brothers felt that we should be treated as brothers? They say we are ignorant. But have we had a complete chance to develop our ability to the utmost?

Where we have strived to build, they have torn down. Where we have tried to better education, they destroyed our purpose.

Yes, we are, as some would say, bound or devoted to live off the Caucasians. But can the devoted do without the persons who are devoting?

Now ask yourself, "Why does all this supremacy exist?"

During the time of slavery in America, the white Lords told their slaves that they (the lords) were supreme over them. Yet they revolted then and we, the free, are still revolting. Yes, we have the so called lords of the manor existing today, but do you and I believe that they are supreme?

Some are too blind to let life exist among both races.

When all of these wealthy processions are gone, to whom shall our brothers turn?

They, our brothers, have converted the words of the Supreme Being to meet their own needs.

Yea, they are sinners, great sinners, but as it is, we are all sinful.

These acts which I have discussed are not indicated by all our brothers, for some have come to realize our position, and theirs, to meet the world's standards.

So friends, citizens and statesmen, think of your position in society and help to show our brothers where they are wrong and where their forefathers were also wrong.

Let's not condemn the whole world for a few people's acts.

Thank You.

Anonymous

You're Free to Have Some Fun Tongue Twister

Theophilus Thistle, the successful thistle sifter, while sifting a sifterful of unsifted thistles, thrust three thousand thistles through the thick of his thumb.

Advice to the successful thistle sifter; never thrust three thousand unsifted thistles through the thick of your thumb.

Success to the successful thistle sifter.

Perceta Rollins

Freedom Star (Meridian, MS)

The Freedom Star was published by students attending the Meridian Freedom School. Although Hattiesburg was known as the "Mecca of the Freedom School world," Meridian actually had the largest single Freedom School, regularly drawing over two hundred students per day. If Hattiesburg was the Freedom School world's "Mecca," then Meridian was its epicenter. Meridian Freedom School students were among the most visible Freedom School leaders in the state and played major roles in organizing and leading the short-lived Mississippi Student Union (MSU). Because of its size and active student body, Meridian was chosen as the site of the Freedom School Convention that convened between August 6 and 8. Opening on the night of murdered activist and Meridian native James Chaney's funeral, the Freedom School Convention brought together representatives from dozens of schools across the state. The students shared ideas, formed the MSU, and welcomed a powerful slate of guest speakers that included A. Philip Randolph, Bob Moses, and Staughton Lynd. Meridian Freedom School leaders used the Freedom Star to organize the convention, using the paper to request housing, plan activities, and later report on the convention. The de facto class president of the Meridian Freedom Schools, a seventeen-year-old student named Roscoe Jones, still lives in Meridian and is active in that community.

July 23, 1964

Meridian to Host Freedom School Convention

On the weekend of the 7–9 of August, Meridian Freedom School is to be the host for the convention of all the Freedom Schools across the state. Each of the schools will be sending approximately three delegates to find housing for 75 students and 25 coordinators. If you would be willing to put up one or two of the students in your home please call 402-1045.

Details of the convention will be announced later; they are being worked out this weekend by delegates from the various schools at a meeting in Jackson.

Rev. King to Visit Meridian

This Friday, July 14, Meridian will be honored by a very important visitor. The Rev. Martin Luther King will be here to speak in behalf of the Summer Project. We will speak in the First Union and St. John Baptist Church; both meetings will begin at 7:30. We urge that everyone attend these meetings.

We also urge that anyone over 21 years of age who has not yet Freedom Registered do so immediately. Any questions will be gladly answered at the COFO office—462-6103.

Statewide Freedom School Softball League to Be Formed

Our Meridian Freedom School will be entering a team in the statewide softball league this summer. The games will be held every Saturday at the different school in the state. It is hoped that everyone will support our team and help us to win the championship.

Interview with Steve S.

Meridian Freedom reporter Fatu. interviewed busy Steve S. the other morning as he was on his way to class. Fat was interested in finding out Steve's impressions of Meridian after coming here from New York City.

She asked Steve how the police force in New York differed from that in New York. He answered that he felt that the Meridian police represented only the white person; he added that if he took a wrong turn in a Negro neighborhood in New York the police would probably simply stop him and help him find his way, but when the same situation occurs in

Mississippi, the police ask you where you are going and what you want. Steve did say that he couldn't speak about all the police in Mississippi.

Next Fat asked how Steve felt about teaching Negroes. He answered that he felt wonderful; he said that he had heard that the children here wouldn't accept white teachers from the North because they were used to the Southern whites. He also said that he was glad to be teaching because he felt very strongly about the fact that the people here are being denied many rights which are due to them.

Two Interviews with the Famous Ronnie De S.

Q. I want to ask you something about your life in England. Can you describe what kind of homes you live in and how different was your life in England from what it is in the U.S.?

A. In many English towns there are long rows of houses that all look the same; They are all made of red bricks and the fog has made them gray. It nearly always rains in England, so that people don't sit out on porches like they do here. In England most people don't have cars, many people ride public transportation. When I left England two years ago there were only two channels on TV, one of them was commercial, like the ones here, but the other is publicly owned and has no commercials at all.

Ben C.

Q. How do you feel about teaching Negroes here in Meridian?

A. I feel that I am down here to hasten the day when no one will talk any more about "teaching Negroes" or "teaching whites," but just teaching people. I am here to <u>agitate</u> among Negroes, but to teach people.

Q. How do you like your students?

A. Love them, especially the pretty ones. And the clever ones. They are just about all pretty and clever—therefore I love them all.

Q. In what ways is Meridian different form your home town?

A. 1. Hotter
   2. Wetter.
   3. Nastier
   4. Much the same.
   5. Don't have a home town anyway.

Q. Who the h— are you anyway?

A. Ronnie de S. and who the h— are you?

Q. Shirley H.

I Am a Negro

I am a Negro and proud of its color too,
If you were a Negro wouldn't you?
I am glad of just what I am now
To be and to do things I know how.
I'm glad to be a Negro so happy and gay
To grow stronger day by day.
I am a Negro and I want to be free as any other child,
To wander about the house and the woods and be wild.
I want to be Free, Free, Free.

Rosalyn W.

How I See Myself at "21" or Over

My aim in life is to be a lawyer. There are not enough Negro lawyers in Mississippi defending their fellow brothers and sisters.

Some people living in Mississippi leave after or before they finish school. I do not see myself in some fancy mansion nor do I see myself living in the scums of places. I just want to live in a decent home living in the neighborhood with people. When I say people I mean both black and white. I do not believe in segregation. I want to help people. To stop this police brutality. I see myself as a decent, respectable citizen. I want to be a nice person. And I would like for people to treat me the same way. If I do be a lawyer or whatever my profession will be, I will not marry until I finish school, grade and law school, and have a job. I mean a good job. Not babysitting or housekeeping.

No I do not plan to leave Mississippi. To help others. I want to look as well as be respectful. Although looks don't mean everything. It's what you know. It's the work that you do and your aim in life. If you lead a good clean life, people will respect you no matter how you look.

With this closing I will say that "I will strive to do the best that I can."

Anonymous

Because I'm Black

Sometimes I ask myself why did I have to be born black?
And there are times when I feel as if I want to turn back!
But then I ask myself again didn't God put me here for a purpose? Then I know that's why I'm not going to be satisfied within the Negro circle.

Just because God saw fit to paint me black; I'm the one that always sits in the back.
I'm a man and I want to be treated as a man and not as a left hand.

One day God's gonna lift his hand over this great land, I want to be a left or a right but a man.

I hope we all be around when God brings the high and mighty to the ground.

Ruth P.

Interview with Betty L.

Q. In what ways is Meridian different from your home town?

A. The main difference is that my home town—New York City—is in the North and Meridian is in the South. In New York, being a Northern city, problems of racial injustice do exist but are more subtle and more difficult to grab onto and deal with. In Meridian, being a Southern city, these problems are more blatant and out in the open. But I also feel that here there is a great deal of spirit, hope, and strength with which to struggle against these injustices. Once changes can occur here perhaps my own home town and the rest of the nation can change also.

Q. How do you like teaching in the Freedom School?

A. I've found teaching in the Freedom School very exciting and rewarding. The students are alert and interested—the future leaders of the Mississippi Freedom Movement. Their understanding of the problems that they and all of us face is amazing. Together we have all grown in our understanding of each other and of the tasks that still need to be fulfilled. I hope that we can try to apply our understanding and actively work toward realizing our goals.

Freedom

Freedom means to be free,
And buzz around like the bumble bee.
To be Free, Free, Free.

To fly up in the air,
And go to places everywhere.
To be Free, Free, Free.

To have your rights,
To roam the streets at night.
To be Free, Free, Free.

To be free like a bird in the air,
To walk through the forest so mild and fair.
To be Free, Free, Free.

Rosalyn W.

As a Negro I Want to Be

As a Negro I want to be equal as every man
Able to walk hand and hand,
Able to live a happy life
As every other man's children and wife.

I want to be equal and superior
To those men that call Negroes inferior
I want to prove I'm just as good
As any race and white man should.

As a Negro I want to be
As any other man on this earth, free;
For I am like a white man, given a birth,
Both black men and white men are parts of this earth.

Sadie Yvonne C.

Freedom Story

Once upon a time there were two little girls, talking one day. These girls were Negro children who had recently moved from big cities like California, New York, Chicago, and other places. They were talking about how different Mississippi was from any place else they knew of.

So one little girl said to the other one, Why is Mississippi so different from other places? In other places you can go anywhere you want to. To different movie theaters, drive in theaters, and different stores. The other girl said, That's what I wanted to know. In Mississippi I don't see any places that are Integrated. Nothing but white people go to places down here. The two girls talked a long, long time. Then they finally went home. When one of the girls got there her mother told her that they would be moving back to New York. Because she didn't like it down here at all. The Negroes didn't have hardly any places to go to. The next day this family moved and went back to their own house and didn't ever come back.

Rosalyn W.

◆   ◆   ◆

July 30, 1964

Report from Jackson

By Lelia Jean Waterhouse

On arriving in Jackson July 25, 1964, Rose, Sarbie, Dorothy and I along with our coordinator Mark went to plan the convention. First we elected officers; they were:

Chairman—Joyce Brown, McComb.
Asst. Chairman—Roscoe Jones, Meridian.
Secretary—Lelia Waterhouse, Meridian.
Asst. Sec.—Delmas Henderson, Columbus.

Treasurer—Malcolm Taylor, Vicksburg.
Asst. Treasurer—Dorothy Gathright, Meridian.

Second we outlined the program for the Convention:
Saturday—

    9:30–10:00 Registration and Credentials.
    10:00–11:00 General Assembly
    11:00–12:30 Committees 1–4.
    12:30–1:30 Lunch at the School.
    1:30–3:00 Committees 1–4.
    3:00–6:00 General Assembly.

First Keynote Address: Vote on resolutions from Committees.

(Suggested Keynote Speakers, Bob Moses, Fanny Lou Hamer.)
    6:00–8:00 Dinner at home
    8:00 Free Southern Theater.

Sunday—

The program will be similar to Saturday.

The suggested platform areas for the Committees were: education, public accommodations, voting, housing, health, federal aid, etc.

The trip to Jackson was very enjoyable and I know that everyone had a nice time.

FREEDOM DEMOCRATIC PARTY TO HOLD DISTRICT MEETING

The Fourth District Meeting of the Freedom Democratic Party will be held here at the School on Sunday, August 2, at 3 p.m. EVERYONE IS URGED TO ATTEND.

Places Are Still Needed for Convention Delegates

Any one who can possibly house and/or feed one or more of the delegates to the Freedom School Convention on August 7, 8, 9, is asked to call the school—482-1845.

This is very important as we are expecting over 100 people. Most of the delegates will be Negro Freedom School students from across the state, and the rest will be coordinators, most of whom will be white. It is very important that we find housing for these people so please try to let us know.

The House of Liberty

I came not for fortune, nor for fame,
I seek not to add glory to an unknown name.
I did not come under the shadow of night,
I came by day to fight for what's right.
I shan't let fear, my monstrous foe,
Conquer my soul with threat and woe.
Here I have come and here I shall stay,
And no amount of fear, my determination can sway.

I asked for your churches, and you turned me down,
But I'll do my work if I have to do it on the ground;
You will not speak for fear of being heard,
So you crawl in your shell and say, "Do not disturb."
You think because you've turned me away,
You've protected yourself for another day.

But tomorrow surely must come,
And your enemy will still be there with the rising sun;
He'll be there tomorrow as all tomorrows in the past,
And he'll follow you into the future if you let him pass.
You've turned me down to humor him,
Ah: Your face is sad and grim.
For even tho' your help I ask,
Even without it, I'll finish my task.

In a bombed house I have to teach my school,
Because I believe all men should live by the Golden
Rule.
To a bombed house your children must come,
Because of your fear of a bomb.
And because you've let your fear conquer your
Soul.
In this bombed house these minds I must try to
Mold;
I must try to teach them to stand tall and be
A man,
When you their parents have cowered down and refused
To take a stand.

Joyce Brown
McComb Freedom School

Declaration of Independence

By the students of the St. John's Methodist Church Freedom
School, Palmer's Crossing, Hattiesburg, Miss.

In this course of human events, it has become necessary for the
Negro people to break away from the customs which have made
it very difficult for the Negro to get his God-given rights. We,
as citizens of Mississippi, do hereby state that all people should
have the right to petition, to assemble, and to use public places.
We also have the right to life, liberty, and to seek happiness.

The government has no right to make or to change laws without the consent of the people. No government has the right to
take the law into its own hands. All people as citizens have the
right to impeach the government when their rights are being
taken away.

All voters elect persons to the government. Everyone must
vote to elect the person of his choice; so we hereby state that

all persons of twenty-one years of age, whether black, white, or yellow, have the right to elect the persons of their choice; and if these persons do not carry out the will of the people, they have the right to alter or abolish the government.

The Negro does not have the right to petition the government for a redress of these grievances:

For equal opportunity.
For better schools and equipment.
For better recreation facilities.
For more public libraries.
For schools for the mentally ill.
For more and better senior colleges.
For better roads in the Negro communities.
For training schools in the State of Mississippi.
For more Negro policemen.
For more guarantee of fair circuit clerks.
For integration in colleges and schools.

The government has made it possible for the white man to have a mock trial in the case of a Negro's death.

The government has refused to make laws for the public good.
The government has used police brutality.
The government has imposed taxes upon us without representation.
The government has refused to give the Negroes the right to go into public places.
The government has marked our registration forms unfairly.

We, therefore, the Negroes of Mississippi assembled, appeal to the government of the state, that no man is free until all men are free. We so hereby declare independence from the unjust laws of Mississippi which conflict with the United States Constitution.

Freedom Star (Meridian, MS)

Student Editorial

CHARITY ONLY: NOT WANTED

Every Negro who has done any amount of traveling in the past few years (since the white man discovered the Negro) can well appreciate the position of a colored traveler sitting on a train with a white man commiserating with him. Attempting to read his paper to find out, perhaps, if Willie Mays is still hitting above .400 or if the invasion of Cuba is really going to come off, he finds himself collared by a loquacious, conscience stricken Caucasian who is bent on solving the entire race problem by one personal act of charity. This position would have been just as effective with any number of outlines that could be readily supplied by almost any Negro—"For the last time, I don't want to marry your daughter," or "For the last time I don't want to go home with you for dinner," or perhaps, "For the last time I don't want a job in your front office."

Like the jokes told by Dick Gregory, Nipsey Russell and Godfrey Cambridge, this situation has a bitter humor that brings instant laughter but yet makes a lasting and serious psychological point—the white man is still condescending to offer only charity.

Emma P.

Notice to Students of the Meridian Freedom School

The FREEDOM STAR is your paper and any articles which you would like to submit for publication are welcome; we are only sorry that we cannot print all of the poems, articles, and stories which are handed in to us. Some of the things that were submitted too late for this issue will appear in the next.

◆　◆　◆

Freedom Star (Meridian, MS)

August 19, 1964

The Freedom School Convention of August 7–10, 1964: Three Reports

The convention started Saturday morning at 9:30am with the chairman opening the meeting by introducing the officers and telling where each officer was from. Members of the executive committee were Joyce Brown, Chairman (McComb); Roscoe Jones, Assistant Chairman (Meridian); Lelia Jean Waterhouse, Secretary (Meridian); Delmas Henderson, Assistant Secretary (Columbus); Malcolm Taylor, Treasurer (Vicksburg); Dorothy Gathright, Assistant treasurer (Meridian).

On Saturday there were four committees and workshops that met. They were Public Accommodations, Housing, Foreign Affairs, and Medical Care. On Sunday the four committees and workshops that met were Federal Aid, City Maintenance, Job Opportunities, and Voter Registration.

It was moved that a copy of the entire platform be sent to each mayor in the state of Mississippi, the Governor, to the state senators and representatives, and the President of the United States. Furthermore, a copy will be sent the Library of Congress for its permanent records.

Lelia Jean Waterhouse

The convention was very nice and enjoyable for everyone. I had a very nice time: it was a great experience for me to attend a convention like this one. The Coordinators and students were very friendly.

Charles Thurman (Greenwood)

On August 7, 1964, the Freedom Schools and the Mississippi Student Union met at the Baptist Seminary for a convention. The convention was very good from the start to finish. There were many Freedom Schools from all over the state to make the convention.

One of the most important things to tell about is the way the different schools talked together to make the convention platform. The students in the convention had one thing in common; we all live in a state where Negroes have very little to say about the ways government is being run.

This is the reason the convention was a great success. The students at the convention have made a great start toward showing Mississippi and the world that the young people of this state are looking out not only for the Negroes, but also for the whites of this "great" state of Mississippi. (By great I mean that Mississippi is telling the other states that it is for the Right and Right alone. This and only this is what this state is doing.)

In closing I would like to say that a copy of the convention platform will be sent to Governor Johnson, the Senate, the Representatives, the Library of Congress, and the President of the United States of America.

Roscoe Jones

Negroes in the United States

We, in the United States, want to belong to our country because each and every citizen in it has a chance to say how he wants his government to be run. We want to feel that we can vote for laws and officials, and that the majority of the voters choose. We want to be free to think and to judge and to choose. We want to be able to accept what most people vote to have.

Linda W.

Letter to the Editor

(Note: The following letter was written by Phil's English class 1B for publication in the <u>Meridian Star</u>, which for some reason, chose not to print it.)

To the Editor:

What does freedom mean to Negroes? The word freedom means to be free and have all the equal rights that belong to each man regardless of race, color, or creed. We were forced to leave Africa; we were born in America, and we should have the rights of any American. We are not treated like human beings. America is not the land of the brave and free. Some Negroes have the same education and skills like any white man but we are denied to have the same jobs.

Our Day Freedom Now

That was our day, June 21, 1964
When our freedom fight began.
Yes, it was Chaney, Schwerner, and Goodman's day, too.
And that's why they died for you and me.
After forty-eight days of struggle they've gotten their peace.
We must now fight for our rights.
We can't let freedom die because Chaney, Schwerner, and
Goodman
Died.
But we must continue the struggle they begun.
Three men's death began our fight
But if three men strengthen the freedom movement
Just think what 20,000 hands can do.
So the best thing we can do for them
Is to love our enemies as well as our friends.
And fight for their freedom as well as our freedom.
What are we going to do?
Fight for "Freedom," That's our aim.

Deseree Page

Interview with Tina Duncan

Q. How is your home different from down here?

A. I come from the San Joaquin Valley in central California—and the weather is very much the same except it is more humid here. The valley is an agricultural area so the towns are quite small and most of the area is covered with grape vines and orange groves and various other kinds of fruit. A little to the south of where I live cotton is grown also.

Q. Are there dogs and cats running around the streets like there are here?

A. Yes.

Q. Do some people burn wood?

A. Yes—in the winter to keep warm.

Q. How does "downtown" look in your town?

A. My home town is very small—and the downtown area consists of only one street. People come there to shop and talk to one another.

Q. Do you think Ronnie is very famous around the school?

A. I have no idea, is he?

Q. Do you like teaching here?

A. I like it very much because most of the students are nice and want to learn.

Q. Do any of your students talk back to you?

A. Sometimes my class gets too noisy—but I quiet them down.

Q. Do you like all of your students?

A. Yes.

Q. Do some houses up where you live look as bad as some down here?

A. Yes—and you'll find this to be true all over the country.

Q. Do they have cows and horses and things in your home town?

A. Yes.

Q. Do you have any sisters or brothers?

A. Yes two brothers 19 and 13 years old.

Pat T.

Freedom News (Palmer's Crossing, MS)

Students attending Freedom Schools held in the Priest's Creek Missionary Baptist Church and St. John's Methodist Church of Palmer's Crossing banded together to produce the Freedom News. A small community
located just outside of Hattiesburg, Palmer's Crossing was home to
some of Mississippi's most enthusiastic and impressive Freedom School
students. Collectively, the Priest's Creek and St. John's Freedom Schools
enjoyed perhaps the best-trained faculty in the entire Freedom School
system. Overwhelmed by the number of students who arrived for classes,
the Palmer's Crossing Freedom School administrators requested addi-
tional teachers to meet their enrollment needs. Many of the new arrivals
were veteran New York City teachers who belonged to the United Federation of Teachers (UFT). As opposed to some Freedom School volunteers
who had never before taught, many UFT members were experienced
educators who had dedicated their lives and careers to instructing young
people. Some had also previously worked with underprivileged African
American youths in northern schools. Another Palmer's Crossing teacher
was a Columbia and Yale University–educated college professor.

As is evidenced in the essays that follow, students in the Palmer's
Crossing Freedom Schools were tremendously excited about their classes
and the movement that was enveloping their community. They used the
African American history lessons to reflect on their ancestors' experience
and dream of a better future for themselves. One of the most significant
contributions made by the students in the Palmer's Crossing Freedom
Schools was their "Declaration of Independence," which was distributed
throughout the state and even reproduced in some of the other Freedom
School newspapers.

July 23, 1964

MFDP Precinct Meeting

The MISSISSIPPI FREEDOM DEMOCRATIC PARTY is the
party that represents <u>all</u> the people in Mississippi. You do not

Freedom News (Palmer's Crossing, MS)

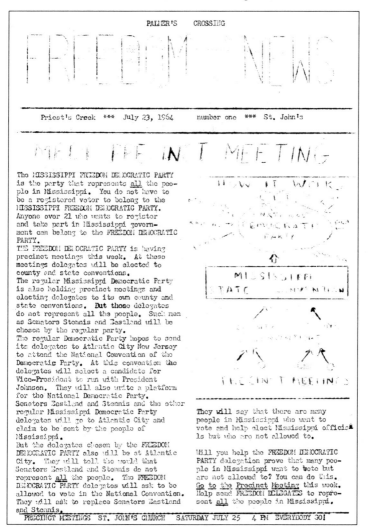

PALMER'S CROSSING

FREEDOM NEWS

Priest's Creek *** July 23, 1964   number one *** St. John's

MEET THE FDP MEETING

The MISSISSIPPI FREEDOM DEMOCRATIC PARTY is the party that represents all the people in Mississippi. You do not have to be a registered voter to belong to the MISSISSIPPI FREEDOM DEMOCRATIC PARTY. Anyone over 21 who wants to register and take part in Mississippi government can belong to the FREEDOM DEMOCRATIC PARTY.

THE FREEDOM DEMOCRATIC PARTY is having precinct meetings this week. At these meetings delegates will be elected to county and state conventions.

The regular Mississippi Democratic Party is also holding precinct meetings and electing delegates to its own county and state conventions. But those delegates do not represent all the people. Such men as Senators Stennis and Eastland will be chosen by the regular party.

The regular Democratic Party hopes to send its delegates to Atlantic City New Jersey to attend the National Convention of the Democratic Party. At this convention the delegates will select a candidate for Vice-President to run with President Johnson. They will also write a platform for the National Democratic Party.

Senators Eastland and Stennis and the other regular Mississippi Democratic Party delegates will go to Atlantic City and claim to be sent by the people of Mississippi.

But the delegates chosen by the FREEDOM DEMOCRATIC PARTY also will be at Atlantic City. They will tell the world that Senators Eastland and Stennis do not represent all the people. The FREEDOM DEMOCRATIC PARTY delegates will ask to be allowed to vote in the National Convention. They will ask to replace Senators Eastland and Stennis.

HOW IT WORKS

FREEDOM DEMOCRATIC PARTY

MISSISSIPPI STATE CONVENTION

PRECINCT MEETINGS

They will say that there are many people in Mississippi who want to vote and help elect Mississippi officials but who are not allowed to.

Will you help the FREEDOM DEMOCRATIC PARTY delegation prove that many people in Mississippi want to vote but are not allowed to? You can do this. Go to the Precinct Meeting this week. Help send FREEDOM DELEGATES to represent all the people in Mississippi.

PRECINCT MEETINGS ST. JOHN'S CHURCH   SATURDAY JULY 25   4 PM EVERYBODY GO!

Masthead of the Palmer's Crossing *Freedom News*.
Courtesy of the McCain Library and Archives, University of Southern Mississippi.

have to be a registered voter to belong to the MISSISSIPPI FREE-DOM DEMOCRATIC PARTY. Anyone over 21 who wants to register and take part in the Mississippi government can belong to the FREEDOM DEMOCRATIC PARTY.

THE FREEDOM DEMOCRATIC PARTY is having precinct monthly meetings this week. At these meetings delegates will be elected to county and state conventions.

The regular Mississippi Democratic Party is also holding precinct meetings and electing delegates to its own county and state conventions. But these delegates do not represent all the people. Such men as Senators Stennis and Eastland will be chosen by the regular party.

The regular Democratic Party hopes to send its delegates to Atlantic City New Jersey to attend the National Convention of the Democratic Party. At this convention the delegates will select a candidate for vice president to run with President Johnson. They will also write a platform for the National Democratic Party.

Senators Eastland and Stennis and the other regular Mississippi Democratic Party delegates will go to Atlantic City and claim to be sent by the people of Mississippi.

But the delegates chosen by the FREEDOM DEMOCRATIC PARTY also will be in Atlantic City. They will tell the world that Senators Eastland and Stennis do not represent all the people. The FREEDOM DEMOCRATIC PARTY delegates will ask to be allowed to vote in the National Convention. They will ask to replace senators Eastland and Stennis.

They will say that there are too many people in Mississippi who want to vote and help elect Mississippi officials but who are not allowed to.

Will you help the FREEDOM DEMOCRATIC PARTY delegation prove that many people in Mississippi want to vote but are not allowed to? You can do this. <u>Go to the Precinct Meeting</u> this week. Help send FREEDOM DELEGATES to represent <u>all</u> the people in Mississippi.

Canvassing

Before you go out canvassing you talk to southernpeople. They tell you that the people will think of you as just another white person exploiting them. The people will tell you that they're going down and say that they agree with you just to get rid of you. They think of you as just another white person telling them, directing, them, what to do.

Most of the Negroes of Mississippi have been in a rut for many years. They think of themselves constantly as a hopeless people. You won't be doing the job you came to do unless you shock them. You don't get anywhere with them unless you're a gadfly. You <u>must</u> be persistent. It's the only way you can have any success in getting the Negroes of Mississippi to act politically.

The most difficult task is not so much getting the people to go down and register to vote as it is of getting them to see themselves as leaders, as acting politically and of getting others to act politically. The Mississippi Project will not succeed until local leaders, with confidence to act in an effective political way, are developed.

If the canvassers sometimes feel that they have been harsh with people trying to get them to go to the courthouse, they get a great deal of satisfaction out of seeing that person who did go down to register has acquired a certain amount of self-respect because he has stood up as a man, in some cases perhaps for the first time in his or her life.

Carolyn M.

***

DON'T TALK POLITICS
Unless you are a registered voter

We Shall Overcome

America is a very wonderful place to live in. It has its advantages and disadvantages.

I have lived in the state of Mississippi for the majority of my life. When I was a child I was very content. As I grew older I began to realize that I was being treated unequal because of the color of my skin.

Now that the Civil rights Law has been passed I pray and hope for a better America, and a better Mississippi in which to live.

Deep down I know that we shall overcome someday. This is my belief and also the belief of my sister and brothers.

I will continue to fight for peace for all Americans "In the name of Freedom."

Theresia C.

Untitled

The reason why I like Freedom School is because the northern teachers came down to Hattiesburg to teach us. I have learned what I didn't learn in other schools, such as Negro history. I wasn't taught Negro history until Negro history week. I have learned that the Irish and Italians were trying to get their freedom too.

I know that the white people are angry because the civil rights laws has passed, but I am very glad because we are able to go to cafes and shows, we will have better school books and most of all we will have the opportunity to go to better schools.

Theola McC.

The Darkness of the Negro Students

Some of the Negro students have been complaining about their teachers. They said their teachers did not give any information about the freeing of their people. The information given to them was false. They teach only what the white man wants us to hear. We have been taught that the white man was responsible for the abolishing of slavery, but that is false. What about the Negro abolitionists?

We have been taught that when the Negroes were free they were helpless. But that is false because they helped themselves by building houses and raising crops.

The reason for my coming out of the darkness is by attending Freedom Schools. At this school both sides of the story are told.

Lynda C.

At Palmer's

The older people of Palmer's and other places are waiting for the younger people, like those from 18 on up.

Yet they think they will stand by and watch our freedom go down the drain. We are the only ones to my thinking who really are free.

Me, I know that they'd rather have Palmer's as it is today. Not me. When we eat at small places in town they watch, telling no. They talk about us behind our backs.

But all the people of the United States understand, we have plenty of people who really care, like those who work for COFO.

Fred T.

In Freedom School

The Negro all his life has been considered nobody. Thanks to the movement that has taken place here in Hattiesburg; some of the Negroes have begun to see the light. What I mean by this is, we know our rights as a Negro or should I say as a human being.

In freedom school I have learned about my race, and how we once were. I have lived in Hattiesburg seventeen years, which is all my life, and I wasn't taught the truth until someone taught me like the people who came for that purpose. Thank God and thank these people for waking up the Negroes in America.

Alberta McC.

Untitled

I like to go to the Freedom School. You will like it too. If you want to come and don't have a way, let us know.

I think we should all have our equal rights. We Negroes have been beaten, but we will never turn back until we get what belongs to us.

We just want what belongs to us. We don't want anything else. I think we as Negroes ought to have the right to vote for justice, equal rights, freedom, jobs, we need better books to read. In the stores uptown and down here we have to pay tax. That is a crying shame.

God is looking down on people now. We try to hide things from people, but we can't hide things from God. We pay tax. I think we should have a right to vote. All of our colored men are getting beaten and put in jail. That is unfair I think, don't you?

Rita Mae C. Age 11.

Letters about Slavery

Some Negroes might say that they are free, but no man is free until all men are free. I am not a free woman yet, I am a salve. I know what it is like to be a slave. My people were sold like animals. Slavery should be abolished because I feel that all men should have equal rights.

Just put yourself in my people's place for a moment. You're a slave, traveling for nearly three to four months. You're hot, tired, hungry and thirsty and your family has been taken away from you. Some of you would rather commit suicide than face up to all this tormenting as my people did.

America might be the land of opportunity, butnot for the Negro period. Slavery should be abolished because the Negroes have been mistreated far too long. Slavery should be abolished because it degrades you as a fellow man. Abolish Slavery!

Look deep into your hearts, souls adnd minds. Ask this question, are the Negroes treated just like the white people? Set the Negroes free, we ought to be free as well as you. And we will be period.

Remember, without freedom there can be no civilized America and without freedom there can be no lasting peace.

Judie F.

Letters about Slavery

I come here today not to speak for myself but for all others who are hold in the bondage of slavery. You and law enforcers have forced us to work in your fields for little or nothing. You have wiped us when we make a mistake. You have spat on us, kicked us and called us dirty names.

Even while we slave in your fields you forbid us to talk to one another. We make up and sing songs to pass the time and let the others know what we are planning. You've taken away the right to worship from us. We steal away to caves when we get a chance. And we put a wash pot in the entrance to drown our voices.

We have appealed to you in many cases asking you to abolish slavery. Do you as humans think that it is honorable to own humans? To you today I say, we Negroes are of right and we ought to be free.

This Magnolia state is not a soft fragrant flower but rather a deoderized skunk. Your great wall is cracking and crumbling to pieces. When it breaks we'll be free; and when it does, Mississippi will be civilized and peaceful. There can be no external peace until all men are free.

Judy G. Age 12

Letters about Slavery

Ladies and gentlemen I am here today to discuss the abolishing of slavery. I ask you to look into the depth of your hearts would you like to be a slave? I know the answer is no because you would want to have some responsibility.

Do you know the difference between slaves and a man? A slave is a person who makes more money for the white man with less expenses. A man is someone who stands up for his right.

America is suppose to be the land of the free. Do you call slavery free? Lif, liberty and toseek happiness. Does the Negro have life, liberty and the right to seek happiness?

The Negro to the white man is no more than an animal. He the Negro does not own anything so this makes him feel that he is nothing. To be a man you must have self-respect.

This the white man thought the Negro did not have. If this were so do you think that there would be as many slave revolts as there are? Do you think such people as
Frederick Douglas
Harriet Tubman
Sojurner Truth
Nat Turner
Denmark Vassey
Joseph Cinques
Thought of the Negro as nothing?

I ask you again to put yourselves in the Negroes place. You are separated from your family, you could not say about the way you are treated, no responsibility but work in the fields. It is left up to us, the people here, to abolish slavery.

Charles C.

Letters about Slavery

And we put a wash pot in the entrance to drown our voices.

We have appealed to you in many cases asking you to abolish slavery. Do you as humans think it's honorable to own humans?

To you today I say, we Negroes are of right and we ought to be free.

This Magnolia state is not a soft fragrant flower but rather a deoderized skunk. Your great white wall is cracking and crumbling to peices. When it breaks we'll be free; and when it does, Mississippi will be civilized and peaceful. There can be no external peace until all men are free.

Judy G. Age 12

What I Would Like to See Happen for the Negro in America

For the Negro in America I would like to see things happen. I not only think but know there is going to be a lot of things happening. I would like very much to see the Negro in America keep on pushing for what belongs to them.

The people in America will see it happen. They'll see the Negroes sit-in and stand-in for their rights.

I would like to see the people that are afraid understand what the word freedom means. And unchain themselves from fear. I would like to see the Negro people get the spirit. I would like to see the Negro people respected by white man.

It will happen and it will be known by everyone. The Negroes will also gain equal job opportunities. Things are going to change and happen and we're going to make them happen. We're going to make the Negro people understand that freedom isn't just for one man but for all men.

Unauthored

Man on the Street Interviews

George Cillispe:

I have never been to freedom school because I live in Perry county and we don't have one. I will go if we ever get a school.

It's a wise choice to have a Freedom School and you have to <u>keep fighting and don't turn back</u>.

J. W. Sims:

Freedom school is a nice place to go and learn. I believe it will make a change.

Mrs. D. Sullivan:

I think Freedom School is a swell idea. I will send my children to the Community School. I can't go because I don't have a babysitter.

Mrs. H. J. McGee:

I'm glad these white people came here to help the Negroes because that's what we need. If we have to fight for our rights, then FIGHT.

Mrs. O. Moncure:

I think the Freedom School is good. And I think the Negroes should cooperate and go, to register to vote. I don't think any colored person should oppose it.

Interviewing By: Diane and Carolyn M.

Untitled

We the people are going to make it happen. In order to make it happen, we've got to keep the movement going.

We're going to make Negro people understand what should happen and what the movement is. I'm going to. Are you?

Ann C.

Thoughts of the Future

I WOULD LIKE very much to see the Negroes in America treated as they were human. I would like to see the Negro have equality; equality of their surroundings, their ability to be a man in the eye-sight of others, meaning the opposite race.

I WOULD LIKE to see those things happen, and with a determined mind, will see these things common and others too. I feel as if I'll see these things regardless of what the future holds for me. And if it is God's will that I see those things, I will.

I WANT very much to see the reaction of the Negroes when they get their freedom and I'd like to see the Negroes realized that freedom lies waiting for them. I'd like to see them keep going and never turn back.

I WOULD LIKE to see the Negro understand their problems as individuals which is one of the most important things. Especially illiteracy. A few months from now and we will have no excuse for such as illiteracy because the movement has taken another step forward to eliminate illiteracy.

I BELIEVE that we will continue the movement until we get our freedom; and when we get our freedom I wonder if we will recognize it or if it will pass us by.

I WOULD LIKE to live to see the Negroes uphold the spirit of the movement in activities, have new ideas, not depend on the high official men in office, take direct action and get their freedom. I mean really get their freedom.

Curtis D.

Our Teachers

ST. JOHN
   Doug—South Bend, Indiana
   Stan—New York City
   Jean—New York City
   Greg—New Jersey
   Cornelia—Madison Wisconsin

PRIEST CREEK
   Joe—Kalamazoo, Michigan
   Sandy—New York City
   Marie—Wooster, Massachusetts
   George—New York City

Second Session of Freedom Schools to Begin on July 29

The second three-week session of freedom school will begin Wednesday July 29. They will be located at St. John Methodist Church and Priest Creek Baptist Church in Palmer's Crossing.

As with the first-week session, classes will be held during the morning from 8 to 11 for the younger students, and from 7:30 to 9:30 every evening, Monday through Friday, for adults and those unable to attend morning sessions.

People who have completed one-week session <u>will</u> be permitted to participate in the second session. New students are especially urged to come at this time too.

Registration as well as classes will be held on this day. There will be no registration before this date.

So tell your friends and neighbors to come, and you too. See you there!

Declaration of Independence

PALMER'S CROSSING, HATTIESBURG, MISSISSIPPI
ST. JOHN METHODIST CHURCH

In the course of human events, it has become necessary for the Negro people to break away from the customs which have made it very difficult for the Negro to get his God-given rights. We, as citizens of Mississippi, do hereby state that all people should have the right to petition, to assemble, and to use public places. We also have the right to life, liberty, and to seek happiness.

The government has no right to make or to change laws without the consent of the people. No government has the right to take the law into its own hands. All the people as citizens have the right to impeach the government when their rights are being taken away.

All voters elect persons to the government. Everyone must vote to elect the person of his choice; so we hereby state that all persons of twenty-one years of age, whether black, white, or yellow, have the right to elect the person of their choice; and if this person does not carry out the will of the people, they have the right to alter or abolish the government.

The Negro does not have the right to petition the government for a redress of the grievances:

For equal job opportunity.

For better schools and equipment.

For better recreation facilities.

For more public libraries.

For schools for the mentally ill.

For more and better senior colleges.

For better roads in Negro communities.

For training schools in the State of Mississippi.

For more Negro policemen.

For more guarantee of a fair circuit clerk.

For integration in colleges and schools.

The government has made it possible for the white man to have a mock trial in the case of a Negro's death.

The government has refused to make laws for the public good.

The government has used police brutality.

The government has imposed taxes upon us without representation.

The government has refused to give Negroes the right to go into public places.

The government has marked our registration form unfairly.

We therefore, the Negroes of Mississippi, assembled, appeal to the government of the State, that no man is free until all men are free. We do hereby declare Independence from the unjust laws of Mississippi which conflict with the United States Constitution.

Ruleville Freedom Fighter

Like their nearby counterparts in Drew, Ruleville Freedom School students attended classes in a hotbed of movement activity. Ruleville's project director was Charles McLaurin, the SNCC organizer who was jailed in Drew. The town was also home to the powerful white supremacist Mississippi Senator James Eastland and the legendary movement organizer Mrs. Fannie Lou Hamer, who lived on a plantation just outside of Ruleville and in 1964 became the first African American woman in Mississippi to run for Congress. Partially because of Mrs. Hamer's growing celebrity, Ruleville attracted a great deal of attention. At the beginning of Freedom Summer in Ruleville, four United States congressmen joined a local civil rights rally, singing freedom songs and offering encouragement to local activists.

Ruleville Freedom School students attended classes in the back of the black community's local Freedom House, which was set up by activists specifically for the summer project of 1964. Ruleville's Freedom Schools offered one of the most comprehensive curriculums of any Freedom School in the state. Daily lessons ranged widely and included everything from basic reading modules to instruction in French, first aid, and biology. Ruleville Freedom School students were quickly absorbed into the local movement, joining with other local African Americans in their commitment to dismantle Jim Crow. The ambitious students also began planning their own protests and fashioning new leadership roles, at one point creating their own organization called the Ruleville Student Action Group. Many years after Freedom Summer, former Ruleville Freedom School teacher Wally Roberts remembered his students telling him, "What we want you to do is to help us become freedom fighters. We want to go on picket lines and do protests. Teach us how to do that."[81] The articles published in the Ruleville Freedom Fighter demonstrate the young people's passionate commitment to the Civil Rights Movement.

RULEVILLE FREEDOM FIGHTER   FIRST ISSUE   JULY 1964
This is a paper for and by the Black Folk of Ruleville
This is a paper for Freedom This is a paper by people fighting for Freedom
So that we can tell our i age So that we can tell of our feelings
A paper with the news we want to hear

NOW IS THE TIME. Now--not tomorrow--
but today. The Negro people have
waited too long. Hundreds of years
the Black Folk have been helping build
America. Negroes have worked for
almost nothing. Black Folk have
worked hard. But what have the Negro
people gotten in return? Almost
nothing. The Negro has been robbed of
his share. He still works another
man's land. He still gets only 3
dollars a day. The boss-man makes
most of the money and the Black Folk
do most of the work. This causes a
lot of suffering. Even the children
cannot be given the opportunities they
need. Year after year these things go
on. But all these things must end.
That is why we want to vote. And this
is why some people don't want us to
vote. Because when we vote we're
going to vote in changes. We're going
to vote out the bad officials. We're
going to vote in officials that want
what we want. We're going to vote in
laws to get what we want.

The Power of Non-Violence
When Jesus said, "If a man smite
thee on one cheek, turn to him the
other," he was introducing mankind to
a new way of life - a way of life
which overcomes evil through love. If
a man returns evil for evil, one bad
deed leads to another until one enemy
is destroyed. We have no desire to
destroy those who oppress us. We want
them to understand and respect us.
Therefore, we take it upon ourselves
to love them no matter what they do to
us. We will not give in nor will we
attempt to do violence to them. This
is the beginning of understanding.
Understanding us the stepping stone to
true brotherhood.

by Eddie Johnson

FREEDOM IN THE R IN. The spirit of
the Freedom Movement reached Indianola
Thursday. It was the spirit of the
Ruleville people. Over a hundred
Indianola citizens were part of a mass
meeting in front of Bryants Chapel.
They met in the middle of thunder and
lightning. It rained and they stayed.
They listened to Charles McLaurin.
They felt the meaning of ONE MAN ONE
VOTE. To vote out police brutality;
to vote out officials that keep the
Negro down. To vote in people that care
about people. That care about people
- black and white. They saw a policeman ask to talk to McLaurin. And they
saw McLaurin say wait till I'm finished
talking. And McLaurin went on and
talked. McLaurin went to talk to the
policeman. And they sang Ain't gonna
let no policeman turn us around. Brave
people ready to join you in the fight
for freedom. Let the people in Indianola
and Ruleville stand together for
Freedom. Freedom now.

Masthead of the *Ruleville Freedom Fighter*.
Courtesy of the Wisconsin Historical Society.

July 1964: First Issue

Now Is the Time

Now—not tomorrow—but today. The Negro people have waited too long. Hundreds of years the Black Folk have been helping build America. Negroes have worked for almost nothing. Black folk have worked hard. But what have the Negro people gotten in return? Almost nothing. The Negro has been robbed of his share. He still works another man's land. He still gets only 3 dollars a day. The boss-man makes most of the money and the Black Folk do most of the work. This causes a lot of suffering. Even the children cannot be given the opportunities they need. Year after year these things go on. But all these things must end. That is why we want to vote. And this is why some people don't want us to vote. Because when we vote we're going to vote in changes. We're going to vote out the bad officials. We're going to vote in officials that want what we want. We're going to vote in laws to get what we want.

The Power of Non-Violence

When Jesus said, "If a man smite thee on one cheek, turn to him the other," he was introducing mankind to a new way of life – a way of life which overcomes evil through love. If a man returns evil for evil, one bad deed leads to another until one enemy is destroyed. We have no desire to destroy those who oppress us. We want them to understand and respect us. Therefore we take it upon ourselves to love them no matter what they do to us. We will not give in nor will we attempt to do violence to them. This is the beginning of understanding. Understanding us the stepping stone to true brotherhood.

Eddie Johnson

Freedom in the Rain

The spirit of the Freedom Movement reached Indianola Thursday. It was the spirit of the Ruleville people. Over a hundred Indianola citizens were part of a mass meeting in front of Bryants Chapel. They met in the middle of thunder and lightning. It rained and they stayed. They listened to Charles McLaurin. They felt the meaning of ONE MAN ONE VOTE. To vote out police brutality; to vote out officials that keep the Negro down. To vote in people that care about people. That care about people—black and white. They saw a policeman ask to talk to McLaurin. And McLaurin went on and talked. McLaurin went to talk to the policeman. And they sang Ain't gonna let no policeman turn us around. Brave people ready to join you in the fight for freedom. Let people in Indianola and Ruleville stand together for Freedom. Freedom Now.

The Freedom Movement Grows in Indianola

There was a massive Freedom rally Thursday evening July 23. It was the biggest mass meeting ever held in Indianola. 300 to 500 people came to hear SNCC workers Charles McLaurin and John Harris talk about Freedom. Policeman Nathanial Jack walked into the meeting. The meeting promptly voted to throw Jack out. Angrily Jack drew his gun and said, "I'll shoot somebody, I'll shoot somebody." National Council of Churches representative Allan Levine along with Harris, McLaurin and the brave people of Indianola stood their ground. And policeman Jack had to leave. The police came back later in the meeting but stayed in the background. They were unable to do anything but wait around. McLaurin claimed, "It must be a new day—to have the police stand around and watch. It must be a new day." Just months ago the police would have broken up the meeting. Now that the whole world is watching—they are afraid of us. They know that they are wrong and that we are right. They know that the whole world knows this. Yes, it is a new day. Nathanial Jack should have been fired long ago—Only by standing like men can we finally get rid of him. Yes, it must be a new day. Mr. Giles made a fine speech for Freedom. He said he was going to register and vote. 18 people went to the court house to register Friday. Over 100 young people said they would be attending the new Freedom School Monday. And all of them wanted to go to the Young Peoples Freedom Convention in Meridian two weeks from now. Yes—it must be a new day in Indianola—The Freedom Movement is growing.

Who Makes the Money in Sunflower County

The average family, Black or White, makes $1790 a year. This is almost the worst average in America. Yet 109 families make over $15,000 a year. They have the power in Sunflower County. They are responsible for the low pay that most people get. 1,270 Negro families and 720 White families live on less than $2000 a year. Many of these families live on less than $600 a year. All this is wrong—it must be changed. Right now, the rich people in Sunflower elect the officials to keep things the way they are. When the poorer people vote, they are going to elect new officials. They are going to vote in new laws to make better jobs and more pay.

Precinct Meetings

Freedom Democratic Party Precinct meetings will be held on Friday July 31, 7 P.M. at:

1. Williams Chapel, Ruleville
   for all people in Ruleville area
2. 177 Broadway, Drew
   for all people in Drew area
3. Baptist School
   Jefferson Street, Indianola
   for all people in Indianola area

These meetings are very important for all who want a change in Mississippi, for all who want to have their say. Everyone who is Freedom Registered can vote. Those who haven't Freedom Registered can Freedom Register at the Precinct Meetings. Delegates will be elected in each meeting to go to the county meeting. Statements will be voted on—about what the delegates should say at the county meeting. So come to your precinct meeting. Make sure the right people are elected. Make sure that your voice is heard for Freedom. Bring your friends—it's important for them too.

Plantation Owners Violate Civil Rights Bill Again

Several Negro people working on plantations have lost their jobs or have not received pay in Sunflower County. Why? Because they tried to register to vote in Indianola. The plantation owners do this even though it's illegal. They may soon have to face trial—unless they correct.

Whites Refused Service

Ten white civil rights workers were refused service or eating four different times in two days. When an integrated group walked into the Downtown Motor Inn Dining Room in Greenville, the Negroes were given menus but the whites in the group were told they wouldn't be served. The manager told one of the whites, Tracy Sugarman, that "You'll be welcome back here in your own groups." At another time, three more white civil rights workers were not allowed to be seated at the Mocca Drive-In Restaurant in Ruleville. Four rights workers were ignored when they sat down for service at the City Café in Drew. The Indianola Restaurant has also refused service to civil rights workers. Before the owner knew the people were civil rights workers he offered them a key to the restaurant. The keys are supposed to prevent integration of the restaurant. A few days earlier the owner of the same restaurant harassed and insulted Len Edwards when he was trying to eat breakfast. The owner told Edwards, "I'd rather serve a nigger than serve you." Edwards asked him, "Would you serve a Negro?" The owner replied, "I didn't say that."

Parents Called to Meeting in Drew

Young people were arrested at the Drew Freedom Meeting July 16. Meyer and Chief of Police Floyd told them to meet with officials. Parents were told in the morning to come that afternoon. Such short notice is wrong. They met at City Attorney

Townsend's office. The Attorney and Chief Floyd tried to get papers signed saying that the young Freedom Fighters didn't know what they were doing. But we all know they want their freedom. The Attorney and Chief Floyd told the parents that if they signed the papers they would get a Federal lawyer to represent their kids and the kids would be put on parole. How did the officials know the children would be put on parole? The young Freedom Fighters have not even had a trial. They have not been found guilty. Let's all stand with these young people who bravely say "WE WANT FREEDOM."

Rochester Negroes Tired of Being Kicked Around

Events of the last week in the state of New York indicate that the entire country is beginning to follow the lead of Mississippi in standing up for Freedom Now. The tragic difference is that while the civil rights activity in Mississippi is carefully organized and strongly dedicated to non-violence in direct action, what has exploded in Harlem and in Rochester has been violence. There are reasons for this which people in Mississippi need to understand and perhaps help, by their example, to change.

The Negro in the northern city, living in terribly overcrowded quarters, is depressed by the way his hopes that the north would be Freedomland were so shattered. He is frustrated by having the North be so much like the South he left. He is frustrated by inequality in jobs, housing, education, protection from the law. He is bitter about police brutality. He is depressed by the way his life is. The Negroes in the North who have these frustrations but who have not yet joined the Movement do not really know how to express their frustrations except by violence. And that is why, this summer, northern demonstrations that start out peaceful and non-violent turn out bitter and [word cut off]

There is more to it than this. The situation of the Negro in the North is like the situation of the Negro in the South in another way. All over the country the power in cities and states is owned by a few rich people, a few people who have influence. They are the ones who are the majors, the judges, the chiefs of police in the South. In this North they are the newspaper editors and the presidents of banks and the real estate boards.

Rochester is a good example of this. In the past few years in Rochester leaders have emerged in the Negro community—responsible, tired, serious leaders—like Bob Moses in Mississippi, who see the situation clearly and want to change it non-violently. But all of these leaders were pushed out of Rochester. All of their efforts were called "irresponsible." They couldn't find jobs. Life was made very difficult for them. And so one by one they had to leave Rochester.

Now there is very little Negro leadership in Rochester. But the Negro leaders did not take away the problems and frustrations that the Negro communities feel. So the Negroes, having no responsible leadership, still needed to take action for their freedom. And so now when the newspapers scream about how irresponsible the Negro community

Why Have Students Come to Mississippi?

Why do young men and women come from New York and California to help in the fight for Freedom? The answer is that they do not come down just to help the Mississippi Negro people. They come to help all Americans be free.

For as long as Eastland and Whitton and men like them sit in the Congress of the United States, it hurts all Americans, not just the people of Mississippi. These men vote against medical care for the aged; and when they vote against medical care for the aged, they are powerful enough to keep the bill from being passed. They vote against all bills that would contribute to the health and welfare of the poor of America.

Eastland's votes and his control over votes are harmful to all Americans—black and white, New Yorkers and Mississippians. Mississippi must have Congressmen that care about the American people—about <u>all</u> of the American people.

The men in the Congress of the United States must be elected by all of the people to serve all of the people. The representatives from Mississippi and the people who govern Mississippi must be elected by all Mississippi people, not just by a handful of powerful white people.

The way people are elected now in Mississippi, then, has effects far beyond the state. And so until we have Freedom here in Mississippi there will be no Freedom for the rest of America. This is why students come to fight with the Negro people for Freedom. We are not Free until everyone is Free.

by the Mississippi Summer Volunteers.

Gun Pulled on Rabbi Again

For the second time in two days, a gun was pulled on Rabbi Allan Levine, a National Council of Churches counselor for the Sunflower County Summer Project. Levine and Jeff Sachar, a white summer volunteer, had tried to attend a meeting in Drew where the Mayor, W. O. Williford, was speaking to the parents of the youths arrested or detained at a SNCC voter registration rally on July 15. The group of local Negroes had no lawyer to help them and Levine and Sachar went to the meeting to try to help them. But the Drew Police Chief, Curtis Floyd, pushed the two out of the room and threatened to arrest them. The Rabbi and Jeff left and went to a Billups Service Station to phone in and tell SNCC headquarters what had happened. As Jeff was trying to call, the station attendant asked, "Does this have something to do with civil rights?" and drew a pistol. Jeff and Rabbi Levine left the station quickly. When they tried to tell Chief Floyd what had happened, he told them he was not interested. The FBI has been notified.

At the meeting with the parents, the City Attorney, Mr. Townsend, asked the Drew Negroes to sign statements that their children had nothing to do with the civil rights workers and would not in the future. He warned, "If you fool around with those Communists there will be a lot of bloodshed." All of the parents refused to sign. Charles McLaurin, 23, Negro from Jackson, Mississippi and Sunflower County Summer Project Director, said, "Townsend is making himself the laughing stock of the town for the Negroes. He just doesn't understand what we feel. He so misunderstands Negroes that he actually thought people would sign those statements!"

That's what we're fighting in Mississippi with the Freedom Democratic Party; we're trying to make people with power use power justly and responsibly. Non-violent change in Mississippi, with the Freedom Democratic Party, can be a light that shines all over the North as well as all over the South.

Thirty-three Attempt to Register

Thirty-three Negroes from Ruleville and Drew celebrated the return of local leader Mrs. Fannie Lou Hamer by going to the County Courthouse in Indianola and trying to register. The Registrar let everyone who went to register and there was no time-consuming stalling as there has been before. The total number of persons who have tried to register this summer is now above sixty. Over 350 people have been registered in the Freedom Democratic Party.

White People Harassed Again

A middle-aged couple were only able to talk with Rabbi Allan Devine for half an hour on the evening of July 25th. A Ruleville policeman then drove up and told them "You better not talk with him." It seemed that he was under orders from the Mayor. This has happened before: On July 4th, a local white man had been talking about civil rights with workers at the Community Center when Ruleville police arrested him and charged him with disorderly conduct. Charles McLaurin, SNCC project director for Sunflower County, said, "The incident tonight again indicated that Mayor Dorrough is scared to death that there will be a break in the solid white South; he is afraid that whites talking with us may begin to see how Dorrough and his ilk are ruining Mississippi."

Theater Owner Won't Obey

Charles McLaurin, SNCC project director for Sunflower County, and LaFayette Surney, SNCC project director in Clarksdale, were refused at the main entrance of Honey Theater in Indianola on July 25th. McLaurin told the manager that separate entrances were outlawed by the new bill, but he said "We aren't changing our policy here", and stood with his keys ready to lock the door. McLaurin and Surney then left.

Indianola Registration Continues

On July 24th, 18 Indianola Negroes tried to register. At Thursday's mass meeting, a policeman pulled a pistol. And the Indianola paper and police chief Bryce Alexander have been redbaiting. But this didn't keep the Indianola people from the courthouse. They all took the test with no trouble.

The Ruleville Student Action Group

This group is concerned with freedom, which is the most important thing for us all. This group is for youth, for students, for people who want direct action.

Why WE Want Direct Action

1. We want our school teachers to vote
The teachers at our school are scared to vote because (a) they think they will lose their jobs, and (b) because our principal won't vote, and he won't vote because he makes enough money to support himself and his family.
2. We want better schooling
For instance, in our history classes, we want to be able to speak, not only of what the books say, but of freedom also.

What We Want to Do

1. We will try to make the teachers of our school vote.
2. We will picket the school, and with your help we will surely win.
It is up to you to participate in this program, and with your help they will surrender.
3. We will meet every Wednesday and Friday. If you want to stand up for your rights in this school—

Come to our meeting:

4:30 p.m.—Wednesday and Friday at the community center
7:30 p.m.—Fridays, at Williams Chapel

We Are Encouraging You to Fight for Your Freedom

Eddie Johnson
on behalf of the
Ruleville Student
Action Group

The Freedom Democratic Party is a political party for the Negroes. It is a political party for whites. It welcomes everybody. It is the only political party in Mississippi for both whites and Negroes.

The Freedom Democratic Party is NOT the regular Democratic Party of Mississippi. It is called the Freedom Democratic Party because it stands for the Freedom of the Negro people.

The regular Democratic Party does everything possible to stop Negroes from becoming a part of the political life of Mississippi. It allows only whites to join with it.

The regular Democratic Party does not support the National Democratic Party, the Democratic Party of the entire United States. This is because the National Democratic Party does not favor stopping Negroes from voting.

The Freedom Democratic Party is very different. It tries to do everything possible to have Negroes take part in the political life of Mississippi. It welcomes the Negro people. This new party is also different because it supports the National Democratic Party. It stands for the same things as the National Democratic party.

In the month of August all the Democratic Parties of the US will have a meeting. This is a meeting of the National Democratic Party. If the new Freedom Democratic Party gets enough people to support it, then the meeting in August will support the new political party of Negroes and whites. If the Freedom Democratic Party gets enough people to support it, then the meeting in August will not support the all-white old Democratic Party of Mississippi. The old Democratic Party of Eastland, Stennis, and Gov. Johnson.

This would be a big step forward in the fight for Freedom. A big step forward because the National Democratic Party that meets in August makes a lot of laws for the entire United States. We want laws that are for Freedom. We want this meeting, therefore, to support the new freedom Democratic Party.

The new party is for both whites and Negroes. But right now almost all whites are against this Freedom Party. Support for the Freedom Democratic Party must come from Negroes.

How can Negroes give their support to the new party? How can we have laws for Freedom? We can support the new party by filling out the Freedom Forms. Those are the forms that young people are taking door to door all over Mississippi. Filling out the form shows that Negroes want more than $3 a day pay. Shows that we want equal rights. Shows that we want Freedom. Shows that we want to vote.

Those Freedom Forms are just like the forms used many places up North for people who want to vote. People who have signed the form if they lived up North could vote. The number of forms filled out is one way of showing the number of people who are not allowed to vote just because they live in Mississippi. Of course even more people than those who sign should have the right to vote. These forms are very important because they show to the whole world that we want to vote. They are very important because they show support for the new Freedom Democratic

Party. And this Party needs support if it is to go to the August meeting of all the Democratic Parties.

Nobody in Mississippi sees the names of people who sign with the Freedom Democratic Party. Nobody but people working <u>with</u> the new party of Freedom. Everybody should fill out these forms. Everyone should show that they want Freedom.

The Freedom Democratic Party will hold meetings in Sunflower County. It will hold meetings all over Mississippi. It will elect people to go to a County meeting. It will elect some people to go to a state meeting. People can support the Freedom Democratic Party by going to meetings that are held in their town. Everyone should go to those local meetings.

We must support this new party. It is OUR party. We must work for Freedom. No change comes unless our people <u>work</u> for change. We demand change. We demand freedom.

Fill out a Freedom Form! Support the Freedom Democratic Party of Mississippi.

Freedom Flame (Shaw, MS)

On July 19, 1964, the New York Times ran a story that infuriated African Americans across Mississippi. Among a number of racist and inaccurate statements taken from white civic leaders living near Shaw was a statement from a Cleveland, Mississippi, sheriff who claimed that "95 per cent of our blacks are happy."[82] Organizers in Shaw responded with a letter-writing campaign to the northern paper, giving local people a voice against the oppression. Galvanized in part by the letter-writing campaign, African Americans living in Shaw organized picket lines, boycotts, and mass meetings to protest the very real racism that constantly limited their freedom and economic and political opportunities. Students from the Shaw Freedom Schools played major roles in nearly all local movement activity. The Shaw Freedom Schools were dominated by older teenagers, young people who were standing at the cusp of adulthood and ready to claim leadership roles in their community. These burgeoning leaders organized through the Shaw Freedom School's Freedom Flame and the school's large Mississippi Student Union chapter, which in the late summer of 1964 led a boycott of the local McEvans High School. The leadership that emerged from the Shaw Freedom School helped energize and lead a growing local movement well into the fall of 1964 when the local Freedom School was still holding voter registration classes.

August 5, 1964

M.S.U. Students Score Victory in McEvans High School Boycott

Shaw M.S.U. News

The Shaw Mississippi Student Union is composed of about 75 members. The officers are: President—Aaron German; Vice President—Charles Bonds; Secretary—Mary Crawford; Assistant Secretary—Doris Brown.

There are also four committees, each of these committes has a Chairman; Welfare Committee Chairman—Vinson Flakes;

Program Committee—Rebecca Flakes; Action Committe—Ruby Richard; Membership Committee—Willie Crawford

Hopefully we want to increase our membership. We had some members join our club on our last meeting night. We meet on every Monday night.

We are progressing rapidly, and with the students' cooperation we want to keep the movement going and create a stronger one in the future.

Shaw Parents Organize

Thirty five parents from Shaw are organizing a Parents Association to try to meet with the school board and the teachers of McEvans High School in Shaw. After a discussion Wed. August 4, the problems of inept and oppressive teaching at the local Negro schools, they agreed to try to open negotiations concerning . . . (cont. on pg. 2)

Untitled

The Junior Class of McEvans High School sponsored a spaghetti supper in the cafeteria on Fri. July 31, 1964. Plates were sold to three of the volunteers. They went over to the cafeteria to get their plates and decided to eat there. They were accepted by everyone except the principal. "Oh, no; you don't eat here." He said, "You must see the superintendent first." "Where does he live?" asked Morris Rubin, a summer volunteer. "In Shaw," said Mr. Alexander. "And you expect us to walk over there to ask him if we may eat in the cafeteria?" "That is exactly what I expect," repeated the principal. I'm very disappointed, said Morris, "but I will eat outside." So he and the other volunteers sat outside on the ground and ate.

"Let's boycott the cafeteria!" someone suggested. Right away everyone agreed.

On August 3, 1964, the students boycotted the cafeteria.

Another Shooting

Five volunteer workers coming from Jackson to Shaw, on August 4, had stopped between Louise and Indianola on the highway, because of a flat. As they started to leave, they were shot at by some local whites of Mississippi.

Acknowledgments

As with the Freedom Schools themselves, this book was a community effort only made possible through the contributions of a wide range of activists, archivists, and historians. Numerous Freedom School students, teachers, and organizers helped teach us about the Freedom Schools and the Civil Rights Movement, offered valuable feedback and commentary, and even at times donated copies of Freedom School newspapers or pointed us to their location in archives. We are particularly grateful to Hymethia Washington Thompson, Homer Hill, Eddie James Carthan, Liz Fusco, Wally Roberts, Sanford Siegel, Areyla Mitchell, Herbert Randall, Roscoe Jones, Anthony Harris, Glenda Funchess, Charles Cobb, Dave Dennis, Bob Moses, Staughton Lynd, Sandra Adickes, Hollis Watkins, Heather Booth, Ira Landess, Mark Levy, Paula Pace, Daisy Harris Wade, Joseph Ellin, Stanley Zibulsky, Barbara Schwartzbaum, Colia Clark, and Lawrence Guyot. Many of these extraordinary people have welcomed us into their homes and lives, serving us coffee and tea and giving moments of their time to help us better understand their remarkable histories. Some of these interactions occurred in short spans during conferences or even at times outside of meetings, and surely many of these busy activists have since forgotten about our discussions. But the insights shared by these special individuals have both inspired and educated us. As historians we are grateful for your willingness to share resources, and as citizens we treasure your long-lasting contributions to our society. Without your work and dedication to education and activism, neither the Freedom Schools nor this book would have been possible.

This book was also made possible by the support of dozens of archivists, research assistants, and funding sources. We would particularly like to thank Jennifer Brannock, Cindy Lawler, Diane Ross, Ashley Bowerman, Michael Edmonds, Craig Simpson,

Elaine Hall, Kathryn Hughes, Kevin Schlottmann, James Danky, Cynthia Lewis, Christine Pawley, Jacky Johnson, Curtis Austin, Stephanie Bolivar, Katherine Fleck, and Andy Kraushaar. These people gave hours of their lives helping us find, access, and transcribe the manuscripts. In some cases they worked late into the night and made special exceptions. In others, they gave us places to sleep. We are grateful for your help and hope our appreciation shows through in the care that we have put into this work. We hope you enjoy it as much as we have in producing it. Further thanks go to scholars including Sabrina Strings, Jessica Johnson, Jessie Dunbar, Crystal Sanders, Wesley Hogan, Nan Woodruff, Hasan Jeffries, Jerma Jackson, Heather Williams, Genna Rae McNeil, Stan Thangaraj, Charles Bolton, Michelle Purdy, Harvey Graff, Peg Thoms, Christina Greene, Ken Goings, Kevin Boyle, William Van Deburg, Joseph Arena, Walter Rucker, Ronald Williams II, our editor Craig Gill, and the anonymous reviewers for the University Press of Mississippi for helping us think about the structure of this book and offering valuable comments about ways to improve the introduction.

Finally, we need to thank our sources of funding for this project. These newspapers were found all over the country and we conducted much of the research while in graduate school. Those trips would not have been possible without much-needed financial support from the Ohio State University Department of History, Pennsylvania State University's Africana Research Center, the American Federation of Teachers, the University of Wisconsin–Madison Center for the History of Print Culture in Modern America, and the College of Charleston Department of Teacher Education.

Notes

1. Sue Sephus, "I Have Been to School," *Freedom's Journal*, August 24, 1964, 2, Box 98, Folder 9, The Student Nonviolent Coordinating Committee Records (hereafter, SNCC-King), 1959–1972, The Martin Luther King Jr. Center for Nonviolent Social Change, Atlanta, GA (hereafter, King Center); Affidavits from Ruleville appear in Box 11, Folder 37 of the Mississippi Freedom Democratic Party Papers (MFDP Papers), King Center; Charles Cobb, "Charlie Cobb: The Mississippi Educational Wasteland," Box 2, Folder 13, MFDP Papers; and Joyce Brown, "Houses of Liberty," Box 14, Folder 4, MFDP Papers. For more on Mississippi public schools, see Charles C. Bolton, *The Hardest Deal of All: The Battle Over School Integration in Mississippi, 1870–1980* (Jackson, MS: University Press of Mississippi, 2007).

2. Albert Evans, "Why I Deserve Freedom," *Student Voice of True Light*, July 20, 1964, Box 2, Folder 3, in Ellin (Joseph and Nancy) Freedom Summer Collection (hereafter, Ellin Papers), The University of Southern Mississippi Historical Manuscripts Collection, Hattiesburg, MS (hereafter, USM).

3. "Freedom School Report," July 10, 1964, Box 6, Folder 3, Staughton and Alice Lynd Papers (hereafter, Lynd Papers), Kent State University Libraries Special Collections and Archives, Kent, OH.

4. Vernon Lane Wharton, *The Negro in Mississippi, 1865–1890* (New York: Harper & Row, 1947), 182.

5. Wharton, *The Negro in Mississippi*, 181–198; Bradley G. Bond, ed., *Mississippi: A Documentary History* (Jackson, MS: University Press of Mississippi, 2003), especially 125–145; and Nicholas Lemann, *Redemption: The Last Battle of the Civil War* (New York: Farrar, Straus, and Giroux, 2006).

6. For more on the end of Reconstruction, see W. E. B. Du Bois, *Black Reconstruction in America: An Essay Toward a History of the Part Which Black Folk Played in the Attempt to Reconstruct Democracy in America, 1860–1880* (New York: Russell & Russell, 1935); C. Vann Woodward, *Reunion and Reaction: The Compromise of 1877 and the End of Reconstruction* (New York: Oxford University Press, 1951); and Eric Foner, *Reconstruction: America's Unfinished Revolution, 1863–1877* (New York: Harper & Row, Publishers, 1988). The phrase "Jim Crow" is derived from a minstrel show character in the nineteenth century. Minstrel show performers were often whites who painted their faces black for on-stage stereotypical performances of African Americans. For more on African

Notes

American life in Jim Crow Mississippi, see Neil R. McMillen, *Dark Journey: Black Mississippians in the Age of Jim Crow* (Urbana, IL: University of Illinois Press, 1990).

7. Sir Harry Johnson, *The Negro in the New World* (New York: Johnson Reprint Corporation, 1969, orig., 1910), 440–445. For more on the ways African American slaves learned to read and write, see Heather Williams, *Self-Taught: African American Education in Slavery and Freedom* (Chapel Hill, NC: University of North Carolina Press, 2005); and Janet Sharp Hermann, *The Pursuit of a Dream* (Oxford: Oxford University Press, 1981).

8. For more on black Mississippians' responses to education during and immediately after the Civil War, see Christopher Span, *From Cotton Field to Schoolhouse: African American Education in Mississippi, 1862–1875* (Chapel Hill, NC: University of North Carolina Press, 2009). For more on Reconstruction-era black independent schools, see Christopher M. Span, "Alternative Pedagogy: The Rise of the Private Black Academy in Early Postbellum Mississippi, 1862–1870" in *Chartered Schools: Two Hundred Years of Independent Academies in the United States, 1727–1925*, ed. Nancy Beadie and Kim Tolley (New York: RoutledgeFalmer, 2002).

9. "Mississippi School Law," *Hinds County Gazette*, April 20, 1870, 1; Stuart Grayson Noble, *Forty Years of the Public Schools in Mississippi, With Special Reference to the Education of the Negro* (New York: AMS Press, 1918); Bolton, *The Hardest Deal of All*, especially 3–9; and Span, *From Cotton Field to Schoolhouse*, especially 117–176.

10. *Impeachment Trial of Thomas W. Cardoza, State Superintendent of Education* (Jackson, MS: Power & Barksdale, State Printer, 1876), Mississippi Department of Archives and History (hereafter, MDAH), Jackson, MS; and "The Cardoza Articles," *Hinds County Gazette*, March 15, 1876, 1.

11. Gathright quoted in Bolton, *The Hardest Deal of All*, 9.

12. The salaries of teachers in white schools fell as well, but their pay became increasingly disproportionate to that of black schoolteachers. By 1910, white instructors were earning twice the salary of their African American counterparts. See Wharton, *The Negro in Mississippi*, 246, 249; and Noble, *Forty Years of the Public Schools in Mississippi*, 141–142. For more on the Redeemers' response to public education, see C. Vann Woodward, *Origins of the New South, 1877–1913* (Baton Rouge, LA: Louisiana State University Press, 1971, orig., 1951), especially 51–74.

13. See Bolton, *The Hardest Deal of All*, 10.

14. See Noble, *Forty Years of the Public Schools in Mississippi*, 98–104.

15. Span, *From Cotton Field to Schoolhouse*, 176. African Americans often had to supplement their own schools with private funds because their tax dollars were disproportionately spent on white students, a phenomenon historian James Anderson has dubbed "double-taxation." James D. Anderson, *The Education of*

Blacks in the South, 1860–1935 (Chapel Hill, NC: University of North Carolina Press, 1988), quoted on 156.

16. Wharton, *The Negro in Mississippi*, 199–215, statistic on 201.

17. The Mississippi Constitution of 1890 can be found through the Mississippi History Now website using the following link: http://mshistorynow.mdah.state.ms.us/articles/103/index.php?s=extra&id=270

18. Litwack, *Trouble in Mind*, 108.

19. Bolton, *The Hardest Deal of All*, 3–32. For a firsthand account of attending black public schools in Mississippi, see Anne Moody, *Coming of Age in Mississippi: The Classic Autobiography of Growing Up Poor and Black in the Rural South* (New York: Bantam Dell, 1968).

20. Gladys Noel Bates, interview with Catherine Jannik, December 23, 1996, The University of Southern Mississippi Center for Oral History and Cultural Heritage; Bolton, *The Hardest Deal of All*, 45–60; Edward S. Bishop Sr., interview with Charles Bolton, February 27, 1991; "Community in Which I Live" (Gladys Noel Bates Papers, Box 3, "Speeches and Papers, 1948, 1968, 1991–1992."

21. For more on the NAACP's strategy against segregated education, see Mark Tushnet, *The NAACP's Legal Strategy against Segregated Education, 1925–1950* (Chapel Hill, NC: University of North Carolina Press, 2005); and Michael J. Klarman, *Brown v. Board of Education and the Civil Rights Movement* (New York: Oxford University Press, 2007).

22. Bolton, *The Hardest Deal of All*, 33–95, statistics found on 87.

23. John Dittmer, *Local People: The Struggle for Civil Rights in Mississippi* (Urbana, IL: University of Illinois Press, 1994), especially 1–89. As Charles Payne had pointed out, the involvement of clergy varied widely depending on location. See Charles Payne, *I've Got the Light of Freedom: The Organizing Tradition and the Mississippi Freedom Struggle* (Berkeley, CA: University of California Press, 1995), especially 191–201. For more on Medgar Evers, see Michael Vinson Williams, *Medgar Evers: Mississippi Martyr* (Fayetteville, AR: University of Arkansas Press, 2011).

24. Clayborne Carson, *In Struggle: SNCC and the Black Awakening of the 1960s* (Cambridge, MA: Harvard University Press, 1981), especially 1–110.

25. Charles Cobb, interview with John Rachal, Sept. 21, 1996, transcript, F341.5.M57 vol. 668, University of Southern Mississippi Oral History Program, Hattiesburg, MS. For more on the relationship between the Mississippi movement and the Kennedy administration, see Dittmer, *Local People*, especially 153–157.

26. *LIFE*, June 28, 1963. For more on the volunteers themselves, see Doug McAdam, *Freedom Summer* (New York: Oxford University Press, 1988).

27. For more on the debates and concerns over the involvement of white volunteers, see Dittmer, *Local People*, especially 214–241; and Wesley C. Hogan,

Many Minds, One Heart: SNCC's Dream for a New America (Chapel Hill, NC: University of North Carolina Press, 1997), 143–182.

28. *Census of the Population: 1960, Volume I, Characteristics of the Population: Part 26, Mississippi* (Washington D.C.: Government Printing Office, 1961), 26–118.

29. Upon arriving in Mississippi, dozens of Freedom School teachers wrote letters home describing the often stunning lack of knowledge and educational poverty of their students. See Elizabeth Martinez, ed., *Letters from Mississippi: Reports from Civil Rights Volunteers & Poetry of the 1964 Freedom Summer* (Brookline, MA: Zephyr Press, 2007).

30. Charlie Cobb, "Prospectus for a Summer Freedom School Program," Box 14, Folder 13, MFDP Papers.

31. Jon Hale, "Early Pedagogical Influences on the Mississippi Freedom Schools: Myles Horton and Critical Education in the Deep South," *American Educational History Journal* 34, No. 2 (2007): 315–330. For more on Highlander, see John Glen, *Highlander: No Ordinary School, 1932–1962* (Lexington, KY: University Press of Kentucky, 1988).

32. Myles Horton, *The Long Haul: An Autobiography*, ed. by Judith Kohl and Herbert Kohl (New York: Doubleday, 1990), 99.

33. Payne, *I've Got the Light of Freedom*, 73; and Katherine Mellon Charron, *Freedom's Teacher: The Life of Septima Clark* (Chapel Hill, NC: University of North Carolina Press, 2009).

34. Clare Russell, "A beautician without teacher training: Bernice Robinson, citizenship schools and women in the Civil Rights Movement," *The Sixties*, No. 4 (2011), 1–31.

35. Horton, *The Long Haul*, 99; Charron, *Freedom's Teacher*; and Septima Poinsette Clark and Cynthia Stokes Brown, *Ready from Within: Septima Clark and the Civil Rights Movement* (Navarro, CA: Wild Tree Press, 1986); Clark, "Southern Christian Leadership Conference Citizenship Education Program," Box 10, Folder 9, Myles Horton Papers, State Historical Society of Wisconsin, Madison, WI (hereafter, SHSW); and Howard Zinn, *SNCC: The New Abolitionists* (Boston: Beacon Press, 1964), 66–67.

36. For more on the importance of education in southern black communities, see Charron, *Freedom's Teacher*; Clark and Brown, *Ready from Within*; Constance Curry, *Silver Rights* (Chapel Hill, NC: Algonquin Books, 1995); Vanessa Siddle Walker, *Their Highest Potential: An African American Community in the Segregated South* (Chapel Hill, NC: University of North Carolina Press, 1996); Chana Kai Lee, "Anger, Memory, and Personal Power: Fannie Lou Hamer and Civil Rights Leadership," in *Sisters in the Struggle: African American Women in the Civil Rights–Black Power Movement*, ed. Bettye Collier Thomas and V. P. Franklin (New York: New York University Press, 2001); Kay Mills, *This Little Light of Mine: The Life of Fannie Lou Hamer* (New York: Dutton, 1993); and Barbara

Ransby, *Ella Baker and the Black Freedom Movement: A Radical Democratic Vision* (Chapel Hill, NC: University of North Carolina Press, 2003).

37. Dittmer, *Local People,* especially 112–114 for McComb school; Payne, *I've Got the Light of Freedom,* 125; Jill Titus, *Brown's Battleground: Students, Segregationists, and the Struggle for Justice in Prince Edward County, Virginia* (Chapel Hill, NC: University of North Carolina Press, 2011), 146–150; Boston Freedom Schools," Box 14, Folder 6, MFDP Papers; "Freedom Diploma" and "Freedom School Materials: For Freedom STAY-OUT Feb. 26, 1964," Box 15, Folder 5, MFDP Papers; "Harlem Parents Committee Freedom School Lessons Guide," Box 15, Folder 9, MFDP Papers; "Attendance Falls Off At Freedom Schools," *New York Times,* March 17, 1964; and "Harlem Organizes 'Freedom Schools,'" *New York Times,* October 13, 1963.

38. Sandra Adickes, interview with William Sturkey, July 5, 2010, New Brunswick, NJ, recording in author's possession; and "Participants at the COFO Curriculum Conference," "Curriculum Planning for Summer Project," and "Curriculum Planning for Summer Project" all found in Box 5, Folder 6, MFDP Papers. For more on planning the Freedom School curriculum, see Sandra Adickes, *Legacy of a Freedom School* (New York: Palgrave Macmillan, 2005), especially 23–52. For more on the National Council of Churches and the Civil Rights Movement, see James F. Findlay, Jr., *Church People in the Struggle: The National Council of Churches and the Black Freedom Movement, 1950–1970* (New York: Oxford University Press, 1993).

39. "Participants at the COFO Curriculum Conference," "Curriculum Planning for Summer Project," and "Curriculum Planning for Summer Project" all found in Box 5, Folder 6, MFDP Papers; and Lynd, interview.

40. "Freedom Schools, Curriculum, general," Subgroup D, Appendix A, Reel 67.340,864 SNCC Papers (Sanford, NC: Microfilming Corp. of America, 1982).

41. "Freedom Schools, Curriculum, general," Subgroup D, Appendix A, Reel 67.340,1022, SNCC Papers.

42. Freedom School Curriculum, Box 1, Folder 11, Ellin Papers.

43. Freedom School Curriculum, Box 1, Folder 11, Ellin Papers.

44. Lynd, interview; and "Guide to Negro History, Box 1, Folder 12, Ellin Papers.

45. Staughton Lynd, interview with William Sturkey, December 8, 2009, Niles, OH, recording in author's possession.

46. Stanley Zibulsky, interview with William Sturkey, July 9, 2010, Queens, New York, recording in author's possession.

47. Freedom School Curriculum, Box 1, Folder 11, Ellin Papers.

48. Charles Cobb, "Freedom Schools, Day, Noel, 1964," Subgroup D, Appendix A, Reel 67, File 342, Slide 342, SNCC Papers; "Freedom Schools, Curriculum, general," Subgroup D, Appendix A, Reel 67.340, SNCC Papers; "Prospectus for a

Summer Freedom School Program," Box 14, Folder 13, MFDP Papers; "Freedom Schools, Day, Noel, 1964," Subgroup D, Appendix A, Reel 67, File 342, Slide 342, SNCC Papers; and "Freedom Schools, Curriculum, general," Subgroup D, Appendix A, Reel 67.340, SNCC Papers.

49. Mary Aickin Rothschild, *A Case of Black and White: Northern Volunteers and the Southern Freedom Summers, 1964–1965* (Westport, CT: Greenwood Press, 1982), 97. Also see Seth Cagin and Philip Dray, *We Are Not Afraid: The Story of Goodman, Schwerner, and Chaney, and the Civil Rights Campaign for Mississippi* (New York: Bantam Books, 1991).

50. Memo from President Young to Mr. Keebler, Oxford, OH, May 5, 1964, Box 1, Folder 1, Mississippi Freedom Summer of 1964 Collection (hereafter Miami-FS), Peabody Hall, Miami University Western College Archives, Oxford, OH; "Courses Planned for Rights Drive," *New York Times*, April 4, 1964, 30; Lynd, interview; and Mark Levy, interview with William Sturkey, July 8, 2010, New York City, recording in author's possession.

51. Arthur Reese, "Freedom Schools—Summer 1964," *The Detroit Teacher*, December, 1964, 4; "School Data," Box 1, Folder 4, Harry J. Bowie Papers, 1964–1967, SHSW; Freedom School teacher quoted in Elizabeth Martinez, ed., *Letters from Mississippi: Reports from Civil Rights Volunteers & Poetry of the 1964 Freedom Summer* (Brookline, MA: Zephyr Press, 2007), 108; and Adickes, interview.

52. "Freedom School Data," Box 1, Folder 4, Bowie Papers, SHSW; and Lynd, interview.

53. Adickes, interview; Lynd, interview; Levy, interview; Herbert Randall, interview with William Sturkey, July 6, 2010, Shinnecock Indian Reservation, Southampton, NY, recording in author's possession. For more on the role of local African Americans protecting civil rights activists, see Akinyele Omowale Umoja, *We Will Shoot Back: Armed Resistance in the Mississippi Freedom Movement* (New York: New York University Press, 2013).

54. "Books Needed in Mississippi Freedom Schools," Box 14, Folder 17, MFDP Papers; Adickes, interview; Lynd, interview; "Materials Needed for Mississippi Summer Project," Box 15, Folder 9, MFDP Papers; "Adopt a Freedom School," Box 4, Folder 12, MFDP Papers; letters acknowledging donations can be found in Box 14, Folders 17–19, MFDP Papers; and Adickes, interview.

55. "Freedom Songs," Box 14, Folder 11, MFDP Papers; Lynd, interview; Glenda Funchess, interview with William Sturkey, December 16, 2009, Hattiesburg, MS, transcription in author's possession; "Seeds of Freedom," play by Holly Springs Freedom, Box 17, Folder 6, MFDP Papers; and Anthony Harris, interview with William Sturkey, October 22, 2010, Hattiesburg, MS, recording in author's possession.

56. These general activities are mere examples of the widespread Freedom School student activism. Hundreds of Freedom School reports are available in the collections cited throughout this introduction. For scholarly examinations of Freedom School student activism, see Jon N. Hale, "A History of the Mississippi Freedom Schools, 1954–1965" (Ph.D. diss., University of Illinois at Urbana–Champaign, 2009); William Sturkey, "Houses of Liberty: The Impact of Freedom Schools during SNCC's 1964 Freedom Summer" (master's thesis, University of Wisconsin–Madison, 2007), especially 57–71; and Adickes, *The Legacy of a Freedom School*, especially 55–36.

57. "Meridian to Host Freedom School Convention," *Freedom Star*, July 23, 1964, Box 16, Folder 6, MFDP Papers; Lelia Jean Waterhouse, "Report from Jackson," *Freedom Star*, July 30, 1964, Box 98, Folder 9, SNCC-King; numerous Freedom School Convention reports found in the August 19, 1964, issue of the *Freedom Star*, Box 4, Folder 3, Mark Levy Papers (hereafter, Levy Papers), Queens College, City University of New York Benjamin S. Rosenthal Library Special Collections, Flushing, NY; Joyce Brown quoted in Roscoe Jones, interview with William Sturkey, September 18, 2011, Meridian, MS, recording in author's possession (Mr. Jones was the assistant chairman of the planning committee); and COFO Freedom School Convention Press Release, Box 14, Folder 16, MFDP Papers.

58. COFO Freedom School Convention Press Release, Box 14, Folder 16, MFDP Papers; Memo to "Parents of Freedom School Convention Delegates," Box 101, Folder 3, SNCC-King; Lelia Jean Waterhouse, "The Freedom School Convention of August 7–10, 1964: Three Reports," Box 4, Folder 3, Levy Papers; "1964 Platform of the Mississippi Freedom School Convention," Box 6, Folder 3, Lynd Papers; Jones, interview; Levy, interview; and Lynd, interview. Thanks also to Mark Levy for supplying a spreadsheet containing the names and ages of many of the Freedom School Convention delegates. For more on the murders of Michael Schwerner, James Chaney, and Andrew Goodman, see William Bradford Huie, *Three Lives for Mississippi* (Jackson, MS: University Press of Mississippi, 2000, orig., 1965), 120–121.

59. Jones, interview; and Lynd, interview.

60. Freedom School Curriculum, Box 1, Folder 11, Ellin Papers.

61. Untitled Correspondence from Staughton Lynd, date unknown, Box 6, Folder 3, Lynd Papers; and "Summary of Moss Point COFO Summer Program," Box 6, Folder 2, MFDP Papers.

62. Several activists did produce smaller publications. These included *The Mississippi Free Press*, E. W. Steptoe's *The Informer* in Amite County, P. D. East's *The Petal Paper*, Arrington W. High's *Eagle Eye* in Jackson, and Colia Liddell's *North Jackson Action*. See Julius E. Thompson, *The Black Press in Mississippi*,

1865–1985 (Gainesville: University Press of Florida, 1993); David R. Davies, ed., *The Press and Race : Mississippi Journalists Confront the Movement* (Jackson, MS: University Press of Mississippi, 2001); Susan M. Weill, *In a Madhouse's Din: Civil Rights Coverage by Mississippi's Daily Press, 1948–1968* (Westport, CT: Praeger, 2002); and William Sturkey, "'I Want to Become a Part of History': Freedom Summer, Freedom Schools, and the Freedom News," *The Journal of African American History*, Vol. 95, No. 3–4 (Summer–Fall 2010), 348–368.

63. Judy Walborn, "Dear Staughton, Tom, and Sue," July 7, 1964, Box 14, Folder 17, MFDP Papers; Clarksdale volunteer quoted in Martinez, *Letters from Mississippi*, 114; and "Weekly Report," submitted by Ira Landess, July 25, 1964, Box 1, Folder 4, Bowie Papers, SHSW.

64. Bossie Mae Harring, "The Fight for Freedom," *Drew Freedom Fighter*, July 20, 1964, 1, Box 1, Folder 2, Jerry Tecklin Papers, SHSW.

65. "Notice to Students of the Meridian Freedom School," *Freedom Star*, July 30, 1964, 4, Box 98, Folder 9, SNCC-King; and Rita Mae C., Untitled Essay, *Freedom News*, July 25, 1964, 3, Box 1, Folder 1, Adickes Papers, SHSW.

66. Florence Howe, "Mississippi's Freedom Schools: The Politics of Education," *Harvard Educational Review*, 35 (1965), 155–156; Bolton, *The Hardest Deal of All*, 96–116; "19 Negroes Apply at Canton High," *The Clarion-Ledger*, September 4, 1964; "18 Negroes seeking transfer to Canton," *Hattiesburg American*, September 3, 1964; "Meridian leaders take legal action," *Hattiesburg American*, September 4, 1964; "Integration Sought By Meridian Group," *The Clarion-Ledger*, September 5, 1964; "Canton, Summit Integration Attempts Are Turned Back," *The Clarion-Ledger*, September 9, 1964; "Canton School Turns Back Negro Pupils," *Clarksdale Press Register*, 8 September 1964; "High Schools in Jackson Bar Negroes," *Clarksdale Press Register*, September 10, 1964; Hymethia Washington Thompson, interview with Jon Hale, July 4, 2012, Jackson, MS, transcript in author's possession; and Funchess, interview. For more on "Freedom of Choice," see Bolton, *The Hardest Deal of All*, especially 141–166.

67. See also Jon Hale, "The Student as a Force for Social Change: The Mississippi Freedom Schools and Student Engagement," *The Journal of African American History* 96, no. 3 (Fall, 2011): 325–348; Rothschild, *A Case of Black and White*, 110–115; and "Issaquena M.S.U. Freedom Fighter, August, 1965," Mississippi Student Union Folder, FIS.

68. "Massive School Boycott in Indianola, COFO news release, Freedom Schools," Miscellaneous Folder, FIS.

69. Dittmer, *Local People*, 332; "Massive School Boycott in Indianola, Press Release 22 February 1965," FIS; "The Mississippi Student Union Convention—December 1964," miscellaneous folder, FIS; and "Freedom Fighter: Issaquena MSU," Mississippi Student Union Folder, FIS.

70. http://www.childrensdefense.org/about-us/our-history/.

71. http://www.childrensdefense.org/programs-campaigns/freedom-schools/.

72. LaKersha Smith, "Telling Their Side of the Story: Mississippi Freedom Schools, African Centered Schools and the Educational Development of Black Students" (Ph.D. diss., City University of New York, 2007), especially 77.

73. Gloria Ladson-Billings, "Toward a Theory of Culturally Relevant Teaching," *American Educational Research Journal* 32, No. 3 (Fall 1995): 465–491; and Ladson-Billings, *Dreamkeepers: Successful Teachers of African American Children* (San Francisco: Jossey-Bass Publishers, 1994).

74. Robert P. Moses and Charles E. Cobb, *Radical Equations: Civil Rights from Mississippi to the Algebra Project* (Boston, MA: Beacon Press, 2001), 5.

75. See also Moses and Cobb, *Radical Equations*. The Algebra Project began in Boston but quickly developed strong ties in Jackson, Mississippi, under the guidance of Bob Moses and connections at Brinkley Middle School.

76. Lisa Deer Brown of the McComb Young People's Project, conversation with Jon Hale, July 2, 2012; "Baltimore Algebra Project Stops Juvenile Detention Center," Umar Farooq, *The Nation*, January 24, 2012; and "Algebra Project mobilizes students to protest in honor of National Day of Action to Defend Education," Erin Sullivan, *The Nation*, March 4, 2010. See also Charles Payne, "Organizing: The Youth Shall Lead Them," in *Quality Education as a Constitutional Right*, ed. Theresa Perry, Robert P. Moses, Joan T. Wynee, Ernesto Cortés Jr., and Lisa Delpit (Boston: Beacon Press, 2010), 3–32.

77. Howard Zinn, popular activist and historian, was a Freedom School teacher in Jackson briefly during the summer of 1964. Lisa Deer Brown, conversation; and http://mccomblegacies.org/blog/. The Howard Zinn Education Project was founded to honor his legacy and to continue the struggle to honor and learn from the perspectives of those who historically struggle for equity. The group in McComb connects with the Howard Zinn Education Project and a Teaching For Change grant.

78. Anonymous student quoted in CORE Freedom School brochure, Box 1, Folder 6, Goodman (Jill Wakeman) Civil Rights Collection, USM.

79. Bob Moses quoted in Dittmer, *Local People*, 131.

80. Pam Parker, Freedom School Report, July 18, 1964, Box 17, Folder 6, MFDP Papers.

81. Wally Roberts, interview with author, June 23, 2008; Wally Roberts, "Teaching Freedom," in possession of author, also on www.crmvet.org.

82. David Halberstam, "Rights Workers Embitter Delta," *New York Times*, July 19, 1964, 52.

Index

Index

Index

Index

CPSIA information can be obtained at www.ICGtesting.com
Printed in the USA
BVOW05*2329250115

384740BV00002B/3/P